ACTIVATE YOUR
COSMIC DNA

Discover Your Starseed Family
from the Pleiades, Sirius, Andromeda,
Centaurus, Epsilon Eridani, and Lyra

EVA MARQUEZ

Bear & Company
Rochester, Vermont

Bear & Company
One Park Street
Rochester, Vermont 05767
www.BearandCompanyBooks.com

Bear & Company is a division of Inner Traditions International

Originally published in German in 2018 under the title *DNA-Aktivierung durch die kosmische Familie* by AMRA Verlag
First U.S. edition published in 2022 by Bear & Company

Cataloging-in-Publication Data for this title is available from the Library of Congress

ISBN 978-1-59143-441-2 (print)
ISBN 978-1-59143-442-9 (ebook)

Printed and bound in the United States by Versa Press, Inc.

10 9 8 7 6 5 4 3 2 1

Text design and layout by Debbie Glogover
This book was typeset in Garamond Premier Pro with Gill Sans MT Pro, Harmonique Display and ITC Legacy Sans Std used as display typefaces

To send correspondence to the author of this book, mail a first-class letter to the author c/o Inner Traditions • Bear & Company, One Park Street, Rochester, VT 05767, and we will forward the communication, or contact the author directly at **www.evamarquez.org**.

ACTIVATE YOUR
COSMIC DNA

"*Activate Your Cosmic DNA* is a wonderful, comprehensive book detailing various starseed origins. It's a fabulous resource to identify and learn more about your soul's roots. Eva Marquez shows us how to tap into the wisdom and gifts held in our soul's DNA through the activation practices at the end of each chapter. This book plants the seeds to birth a new level of comfort and love that organically arrives when we intimately connect with our truest selves. For all that we earthlings muster through, there's nothing that catapults us into a 5D frequency faster than connecting with our 'homeland.'"

TAMMY BILLUPS, AUTHOR OF *SOUL HEALING WITH OUR ANIMAL COMPANIONS* AND *ANIMAL SOUL CONTRACTS*

"To banish aggression and evil on Earth, we must awaken our extraterrestrial DNA. *Activate Your Cosmic DNA* begins by telling wonderful stories of the star beings that seeded Lemuria and Atlantis, even takes you on a journey to your stellar home! As these memories awaken within, Eva Marquez proposes that recalling our hybrid star lineages activates cosmic powers in us, and this is not just an idea: Her exercises for awakening our dormant multidimensional abilities are very easy to use and very potent. Her epic story of Lyra, an extraterrestrial civilization that long ago outsourced its mental capabilities to artificial intelligence and was destroyed by greed, is a huge warning to Earth. This is a must-read for anyone who wants to awaken their soul by remembering their cosmic origins."

BARBARA HAND CLOW, AUTHOR OF *THE PLEIADIAN AGENDA*, *ALCHEMY OF NINE DIMENSIONS*, AND *REVELATIONS FROM THE SOURCE*

"*Activate Your Cosmic DNA* reveals insights and techniques designed to empower starseeds who are awakening to their full potential. This book is a great resource for accessing multidimensional consciousness, transformation, and healing."

ANN W. MEZIAN, ARTIST AND FOUNDER OF INNERPATHJOURNEY.COM

"Eva is the real deal, and her life story and body of work are a blessing to all who are on the path of ascension. I breathed deep sighs of recognition upon reading the description for Sirius, my primary lineage. Having experienced Eva's magic personally, it is clear she is acutely attuned to these star cultures. Eva is a pioneer in the exploding field of star ancestry, and her soul is dedicated to bringing these ancient relationships back into the collective consciousness. If you are ready to own your celestial heritage, this book is a must-read."

REV. STEPHANIE RED FEATHER, PH.D., AUTHOR OF
THE EVOLUTIONARY EMPATH AND *EMPATH ACTIVATION CARDS*

"A fabulous book filled with wise information and important guidance. Anyone who is curious about their star ancestry or even about what having star ancestry means will find huge benefits. The descriptions of different starseed characteristics, the powerful uplifting images of various home planets, and the wonderful meditations and healing suggestions are remarkable. Marquez has filled in an essential piece to support us on our current ascension process and illuminate our true history in this high frequency and accessible book. Read it once and you may well want to read it again. I cannot recommend it strongly enough!"

JUDITH CORVIN-BLACKBURN, LCSW, DMIN, AUTHOR OF
ACTIVATING YOUR 5D FREQUENCY

"*Activate Your Cosmic DNA* is an intriguing and inspiring book. If you ever wondered about your star ancestry, then this book is for you. The author's downloads are clear and concise, giving detailed information and exercises to support you in identifying your star origins. A must-have book as we awaken to who we really are!"

CARLEY MATTIMORE, MS, LCPC, COAUTHOR OF
SACRED MESSENGERS OF SHAMANIC AFRICA

"Eva Marquez is a beautiful loving soul who is completely authentic in her channeling and dedicated to bringing Pleiadian wisdom and healing to others. I recommend her work wholeheartedly, especially her latest loving account of how we seeded Earth and our true potential through reactivating our DNA."

SHERYL SITTS, HOLISTIC PRACTITIONER, POSSIBILITIES COACH,
AND HOST OF *EXPLORING POSSIBILITIES PODCAST*

First and foremost dedicated to you, my readers,
because you are amazing!

And dedicated to The Children of the Law of One.
You know who you are!

Contents

✦ ✦ ✦

PART TWO

Understanding

A Note to Our Dear Readers and Supporters of Cosmic Information!

By Pavlina Klemm

It is an honor and a great pleasure for me to write these introductory words for my "cosmic colleague" Eva Marquez. I was so interested in what my light-filled friend had to say about the beautiful planets of the Pleiades that within two days I had read her book!

Eva grew up in the Czech Republic, just like me, even at the same time. Her life story impressed me deeply. We were both sent abroad by the Light World—Eva to the United States and I to Germany—and we both feel it our duty to pass on the cosmic information we receive from the Light World.

Our German publisher, who discovered and accompanied us both so lovingly in the early days of our writing careers, introduced us to each other. We found out that our important "duty" connects us. It is an inner motor that gives us the strength to work again and again on behalf of the process of ascension and to bring the energy and messages of the Light World into our world, with love and understanding in our hearts.

I am really very happy that information from the world of light, which is so important for this time, reaches us both. It helps each of us to know that there is someone else who "ticks" in the same way. The information that we channel makes us understand our essence and our human origin. The Pleiadians, whose messages we pass on to the people, allowed us to discover the power of the present moment. Through their understanding, new gates opened for us, as well as new paths into the future, which we as human beings can influence positively. Yes, we can positively influence our own future—and the future of our world!

Maybe you have already asked yourself where you come from and you've searched for your real origin. Eva's information will help you to find out exactly which characteristics of the different branches of humanity are most likely to apply to you and connect you with your cosmic family.

In this book, we learn so much about the peace-loving extra-terrestrial civilizations and their home planets! They all have a special quality: the Pleiadians are gifted soul healers, the Sirians are carriers of truth and knowledge, and the Andromedans offer new technologies and holistic healing methods. The inhabitants of Centaurus are wise teachers and carry much wisdom within them, the inhabitants of Epsilon Eridani are known for their logical thinking, and the Lyrans are benevolent beings who bring us their forgotten knowledge to which we no longer had access.

From my own experience, I can confirm that kind-hearted people—people like you—on the soul level come from other planets in our universe. They all—you included—bring their light, their love, and their experiences to this world we call Earth. The cosmic souls that incarnated on Earth carry these elements within themselves, and Eva, with the help of the Pleiadians, succeeds in allowing you to get to know yourself better.

She makes clear what connects all cosmic peoples with each other: *cosmic love, and a wonderful frequency of light!*

Every single person on our planet is supported by his or her cosmic family and has a great task to undertake at the moment. Every person is allowed to forgive all beings who ever hurt him or her, including themselves. He or she is allowed to purify their burdens and thereby strengthen their enchanting light. This is how you find your light codes—energetic keys that are of great importance for the further steps of human evolution!

Love and light are stronger than darkness. This is expressed in each of these messages, which show that we can reach the radiant goal with united, positive forces. The most important thing is not to lose faith and to stay in its center, not to allow the widespread frequency of fear to spread. Our peaceful frequency of light draws even more light and even more peaceful beings into our field—human as well as light-filled—and our common power and the common vision of a better future bring loving changes.

With the help of the Pleiadians, Eva has succeeded in describing our past in an excellent way. It is important to know our human past so that we may create a new and better future. We are allowed to draw from what has happened, so that something completely wonderful is created—a planet that is lightened!

The peace-loving extraterrestrial civilizations support us in this process.

I wish you, dear readers, much joy and self-knowledge while reading this book. I hope you discover information that will help you find a light-filled key to your soul and your further steps.

Dear Eva, I wish you much love and perseverance in your future light work!

IN LOVE ~ PAVLINA

PAVLINA KLEMM, born in the Czech Republic and presently living in Germany, is the author of *Lichtbotschaften von den Plejaden* (Light Messages from the Pleiades), a bestselling series consisting of, to date, seven channeled books and ten CDs. She is also the author of the current bestseller *Heilsymbole & Zahlenreihen* (Healing Symbols & Number Series), a workbook for healers, which is also available as a deck of cards. Since her childhood she has been in contact with the spiritual world. She is trained in Quantum Healing, Reconnective Healing according to Eric Pearl, New Homeopathy according to Körbler, and in Russian healing methods. She currently lives and works as a healer and channel medium near Munich.

Acknowledgments

I want to give a special thank-you to all my friends who supported me in my writing and reading my drafts! Writing is one of my passions, but English is my second language so it takes a lot to polish my writing and make sense of what I am trying to say! Thank you so much for putting up with me.

I want to express my deep gratitude for the editing done by Natalie Wells, Mackenzie Macht, and my husband, Tom Marquez, who assisted me in making this book possible. Thank you, thank you, thank you! I would also like to give a big thank-you to my true teacher and friend Ann Wood for all her support and encouragement, and for the final editing of the afterword and recommendations sections.

I'd like to thank everyone at Inner Traditions • Bear & Company for working with me and making this book available to many starseeds.

And I am also grateful to Sheldan Nidle for sharing information in his book *Your Galactic Neighbors,* which opened my spiritual door to conscious communication with various star nations.

Thank you!

Starseed Guide

An Introduction

The Pleiadian star nation is one of the most discussed star nations that we know of. Pleiadians, along with other star nations, seeded the Earth eons ago and their energy is still present today. They never left us, they never gave up on us, and if you clear your mind and focus, you can feel their love in your heart. You can feel their compassion and kindness. Their teachings are here to assist you in remembering who you are. Pleiadians are soul healers. Their closest soul brothers and sisters are Andromedans and Sirians. Often they all join in ceremonies on Sirius B and work in unity to ensure peace across the universe.

Sirians are knowledge keepers. The Akashic Records and the Library of Light are on Sirius B. Andromedans are healers and scientists. They understand the physical matter of the body. Together they create a beautiful trinity of energies that synchronize with the energies of our mind (Sirius), body (Andromeda), and soul (Pleiades).

You, as a starseed, carry the spiritual DNA of your ancestors. You have asked questions over and over. You want to consciously understand who you are and why you feel so different. Being different can be the most amazing thing in your life when you understand yourself, and when you consciously embrace your ancient roots and allow yourself to believe that you are an extraterrestrial being living in a human body!

This conscious knowledge should liberate you; it should feed your soul, not your ego.

You will be reading about various star nations and you may automatically connect with them. When you make a connection, you may ask them to activate your sleeping starseed DNA. If they are your original ancestors, you may experience sudden memories, and your spiritual DNA will be activated. If they are just your galactic neighbors, you might receive their energy imprint. You will be attuned to the energy that will assist you in the highest possible way in your current life.

Writing this book has been quite an experience for me. Over the years I have been collecting notes from starseed readings I have done for friends and clients. I have been looking at and meticulously categorizing similarities that I have found in various starseeds from different star nations. What do they like? What don't they like? What are related experiences in their lives? Slowly, I put the pieces of the puzzle together.

After publishing the first half of this book as an e-book, I was guided to write the second half. I already had a pretty good file on the starseeds from Centaurus and Epsilon Eridani, but I hardly had anything about Lyra. I had all kinds of information in my head, but it was not coming out smoothly on paper. For a while I thought that perhaps this file was not meant to be finished. I also questioned why I felt that I had to group these three together. The answer I received was, "Just go with it and you will see."

While working on my first e-book, my guides shared with me that we should work with three starseed nations at a time. Number three is a magic number. It is a catalyst to new energy and a master manifestor. It represents mind, body, and soul. The power of three is universal.

I could clearly see how the Andromedans, Pleiadians, and Sirians worked together in trinity, but I was not certain about Centaurus, Epsilon Eridani, and Lyra. How did the beings from these latter three star nations all come together? After all, when I started to do starseed readings in 2010 very few people had heard about Centaurus, and for most people, Epsilon Eridani is still unknown today. Lyra was surrounded in controversy on the world of the Internet.

Then one day, sitting in my home office, staring at the trees in my backyard, I felt the Lyrans as if they had just landed in the yard. If you are wondering, they did not actually land. Instead I was experiencing a telepathic connection with them and the information they wanted to share started pouring into my brain. I came to realize that all the time I previously spent gathering and organizing information from the different starseeds had been necessary in order to make this book an effective and informative healing tool. I could not rush it even if I wanted to. I also needed some personal self-growth so that I could share this information without judgment or taking sides. I did not pick these three star nations to group together. They picked each other to work with a long time ago, before they even came to Earth.

Writing this book brought clarity to a past life of mine in Atlantis and I hope it will bring you pieces of your puzzle as well. I believe that understanding other star nations, whether you are from that system or not, helps us put together the missing pieces of our own Earth's history. We are not much different than our ancestors from the stars. We too experienced our ups and downs. Chances are if you are a starseed, you may have visited all six of them. Perhaps you have studied or lived there for a brief moment—or even for a whole lifetime. Now it is time to remember that.

Our memories are refreshed with channeled messages, but also with solid data that has been left for us by our ancient ancestors, for example the Mayan Calendar. Pleiadians guided me, long after 2012, to the work of Barbara Hand Clow who paved the way for starseeds like myself. She was part of the Harmonic Convergence in 1987, the first globally synchronized meditation, perfectly calculated to be set on a rare planetary alignment. Her research on the Mayan Calendar and collaboration with others like her resulted in a global shift that I truly believe gave us a rare opportunity to design a different and better future for humankind. And for this, I am grateful. Barbara is a prime example, and my personal inspiration, of what we can accomplish if we follow our soul's calling. Her nonfiction books, *The Mayan Code, The Pleiadian Agenda,* and others are timeless classics that are filled with ancient knowledge taught by a true teacher. Her fiction books, The Revelation Trilogy, inspired from that same wisdom, stimulate your mind as well as your heart. It is the heart-mind connection, joining emotions and knowledge, that ignites the light through your ancient DNA.

An important part of this book is knowledge of DNA and our history. Lyrans are the oldest beings who contributed to the Earth's population and growth. They are grandfathers of the science of DNA and creators of hybrids (merging the DNA of beings from various star nations). They have strong and determined personalities, like elders who have experienced everything. The Centaurian culture is younger than that of Lyra. When Lyrans migrated to Centaurus they assisted in their development. They are bright, with sweet, comforting, and compassionate personalities and, like young warriors, optimistic that they can fix any problem. Epsilonians are like the glue between those two. They are a pod that holds two peas together. They are master mediators and are also currently close to our Earth and can easily function in the fifth dimension, as can Arcturians.

Since Lyrans and Centaurians have the most experience in merging DNA and genetic experiments they wanted us to fully understand about the genetic experiments that had taken place on Earth. Genetic science was developed by Lyrans in Centaurus and then later these same procedures were used on Earth. The first genetic modification of the body was applied to alien races that were currently living on Earth. It was benevolent and greatly welcomed. The reason was to upgrade alien DNA with earthly biological components to create a healthier body with greater immunity that would thrive in an Earthly environment. Pleiadians shared with me that alien bodies faced many challenges living in a different atmosphere than they were used to.

The second genetic modification, the one that we are still influenced by today, was upgrading primates with extraterrestrial DNA to create human slaves to perform particular tasks. This was done by a group we call Anunnaki (mixture of various extraterrestrial races, Lyrans included). This project was kept secret because it was not approved by the Council of Light and humans came to many as a "surprise baby." Therefore, human beings are hybrids, the human body is a hybrid body, and as starseeds we are incarnating into a vessel that is not really compatible with our star-being consciousness.

However, learning about your star ancestors, and the constellation where you came from, will help you to adjust your starseed self in the human body and develop the abilities of your soul family. In other words, you need to understand your body; you need to embrace the human within and your ancestry to understand who you truly are and what you are capable of before you become an "alien" once again.

Epsilonians bring logic of the heart, and as with the Pleiadians, healing to the soul. Centaurians, like Andromedans, work with healing energies of the physical body. Lyrans have access to ancient records and knowledge of forgotten times, as do the Sirians. Each of these starseeds carries slightly different energy, very different DNA, but the same intention in their soul.

We are their children. They love us unconditionally and they are here for us when we are ready to open to them.

Throughout this book you'll find meditations, practices, and recommendations designed to help you fully awaken your starseed gifts and support you in attaining greater levels of mastery in your life. While some of us feel a close association with one particular star nation, other starseeds consider themselves to be hybrids, carrying DNA from various star systems. We're all part of one vast and interconnected galactic family, so I invite you to explore the suggestions listed after each of the starseed sections. They contain essential guidance on topics such as energy cleansing, connecting with nature, and healing.

May this book empower you on your journey.

Enjoy!

LOVE AND LIGHT ~ EVA

PART ONE

Remembering

Pleiadian Message

Your Star-Seeded History

Life is a great journey. Who decides when it begins and when it ends? Your souls have been around for eons, yet your heart is young and endures only for a certain amount of time. How do you begin to align your physical being, your physical heart, to your everlasting soul and become immortal? Do you want to be immortal in your realm of reality?

Embracing the starseed within you begins with opening the door to the ancient knowledge hidden within your history. Knowledge is power. The power is hidden within the soul. The soul is infinite and the body is just a vessel, good for one lifetime. Imagine if your soul was capable of remembering the extraterrestrial being that you truly are, the galactic lives you led prior to your first incarnation on Earth, and all the abilities that transcend beyond the five basic human senses. Now imagine releasing all this information into your physical body. Will you embrace it or will you be afraid of it?

The knowledge that we offer you in this starseed guide, about your star origin, comes from a level of unconditional *love* for you and all Creation. Since the time of Atlantis, the Pleiadians and other star nations have created a pathway for you to discover who you truly are. We left many clues for you throughout your history. Only you can walk the path and obtain the information you are seeking. By applying your own physical energy to this quest, you activate your soul energy and you are led to the knowledge that will bring more than answers to the questions you are asking.

Always keep asking.

THE POWER OF THREE

Three is a magic number that offers many clues to the past and to the future. It also reveals, in your world, coded messages from ancient aliens, your ancestors. The most important connection of threes is the connection of the Earth (your past energy), yourself (your present energy), and the universe (your future energy). When you become consciously one with all aspects of yourself (past, present, and future), you naturally activate your starseed DNA. It may feel as if you are living in one world and walking in several others. You will start evolving more quickly; however, you will have to walk back and understand your past, and heal your soul traumas so you can return home. What happened on Earth has to be healed on Earth. This is one of the reasons why you keep coming back to Earth.

Seek components of threes, as three is a catalyst, when you are searching for answers. We also like working in groups of three star nations while assisting you to align your mind, body, and soul in perfect harmony.

PLEIADIAN SOUL CALL

We, the Pleiadians, are sending a call, an energy transmission in the form of light codes, to awaken your ancient memories of your star origins.

The original journey to Earth began with us, the Pleiadians. You may call us ancient aliens. We hold a frequency of unconditional love within. Eventually, we also opened the opportunity for various star nations to join us. Slowly, as time went on in the Earth realm, by natural occurrences the frequency of love was lowered to a frequency of fear, and many ancient aliens became stuck in the three-dimensional world of Earth. Over thousands of years they gradually fell into a reincarnation cycle together with deep levels of spiritual coma, and began to believe that being human was their natural life.

Does this remind you of something? Could the ancient aliens be your ancestors? Are you one of them just having a human experience over and over again? By now your guides are standing around you, patiently waiting to make a conscious connection with you. Imagine that you have just arrived at a train station after a long journey around the world. Some places you would like to remember forever and others you would like to forget. You are tired from the journey, you are fully aware of your human body, and you silently wonder, *What awaits me at this station?*

Then you notice someone is waiting for you, which surprises you. That someone may not look like an ordinary human, but he or she holds up a sign with your name and shines from inside out with the most brilliant light of your favorite color. You cannot help but be naturally drawn to this being and once you come closer and look into his or her eyes, or just feel the presence of this being with your heart, you feel something familiar. You remember—you remember a time before you became a human. Your soul and your heart instantly recognize a member of your soul family, your current guide.

Stop and take a deep breath; accept the fact that you are not *just* a human being. Let your emotions express themselves freely. Instantly forgive yourself for having forgotten about your soul family, about your own self. Embrace your guide and allow your own light codes to ignite your whole being. If you wish, you are now ready for the next part of your journey—the part where you learn about your star soul family.

HOW DID WE GET HERE IN THE FIRST PLACE?

Once upon a time you were, we all were, part of the infinite God's energy. Imagine that you were oneness and peace without any separation. You had no form, no physical body; you just were God's (oneness) energy. At some point God allowed your soul energy to separate a little so that you could experience all the wonders of the universe.

You loved it and you became more curious with each discovery. You wanted to experience more and that meant lowering your vibrations bit by bit and separating yourself from the oneness of God. The original separation began as soul groups (picture a cluster of light separating from a big sphere of light). At this phase your soul felt extremely peaceful as you did not yet know the feelings of love, excitement, safety, or fear. Suddenly you became aware that feelings other than those of eternal peace existed, and as a child of the Divine you followed your curiosity.

Fascinated with each new discovery you slowly lowered your vibration more and more until you reached the realm of the Ascended Masters and the angels. You became a light body, and experienced unconditional love and universal wisdom. Spellbound, you wanted to experience the colors and energy of tones and sounds. So you lowered your vibration a little bit more. Then you discovered fifth-dimensional lives and incarnated yourself, in extraterrestrial form, on various planets such as Pleiades, Andromeda, Sirius, Centaurus, Arcturus, and others. It was an exciting and mesmerizing time for you.

When you reached 5D you started to have various emotions. Your soul became aware of your whole self as a form (your current higher self) and you developed identity and personality and you found your soul's purpose. You started to feel needed and you were curious. You also learned you could consciously manifest and control the outcome of certain situations. Over a long period of time you were slowly forgetting about the place where everything was complete, where there was no designated soul purpose, no emotions—there was just peace. Before you left God's oneness you received a gift. Part of God's spark is within your soul, illuminating your path back home when you are ready to return.

Prior to your first incarnation on Earth, your soul spent a considerable amount of time in the 7D, 6D, and 5D realms. You spent so much time in these realms that someone who is able to read energy can recognize the energy imprint of your particular star nations, and pinpoint where you are from. You have incarnated many times into several star nations and your soul strongly identifies with one or more of these nations, their teachings, abilities, philosophies, and way of life.

All this is encoded in your DNA. It is a part of your soul.

RAINBOW BRIDGE

Before you came down to Earth you stopped on a bridge in the fourth dimension. It is a passage from the higher worlds of celestials into the physical world of Earth. It is a place that has past, present, and future energy. What a thrill that was! There were patterns and repetition, and battles of power between the forces of light and dark. You stood on the bridge between 4D and 3D and were captivated by the 3D world of emotions, drama, fear, chaos, jealousy, greed, and power. The emotions were fascinating and you wanted to go down and experience how it would feel to have a physical body. You saw primitive animals and wondered how it would feel to be like them: to have skin, to have fur, to run like a cheetah, to have feathers, to fly like a bird.

Eventually, you were instructed that you could only use the Rainbow Bridge to return to 4D with all your memories, but not allowed to use it to go from 4D to 3D. Instead, you would have to wade across the River of Forgetfulness and forget all you knew of your true origins. You had no idea that you would become stuck in this ongoing loop.

LEMURIA

The first two civilizations on Earth were extraterrestrial civilizations. We begin with Lemuria. Lemuria was a Pleiadian project, an experiment of establishing an extraterrestrial colony in the pristine environment of Earth. The experiment was approved by the Council of Light and the Arcturians were also approached for assistance. Lemuria was highly evolved, spiritually and technically. We experienced lowering our vibration to the Earth's 3D density while having fully opened our energy and our soul consciousness. All of us had the ability to hold 3D, 4D, and 5D vibrations in our body and move between those dimensions.

In coming to Earth we retained our extraterrestrial appearance. We brought many animals with us (for example dolphins and whales), as well as trees and plants from our worlds to help the Earth thrive. Since the Earth realm is a place of duality we had chosen to embrace the feminine energy, and females were the leaders of our tribes. Their intuition synchronized with nature and the universe, and allowed them to be a clear channel of future events. Masculine energy plunged in duality could become corrupted faster than feminine energy. The ego is a masculine energy, and as you have already witnessed, the Earth realm can fire up the ego beyond its limitations. Masculine energy is a great source of physical power and creativity. It is a fire that could be your best friend if properly used or your worst enemy if abused.

We did not create the Earth. The Earth was here prior to our original experiment, seeded with primitive and animal life. It was rich in nature, with abundant rivers and oceans. We were allowed to add our life force to Creation, but we were not allowed to genetically alter it. Everything in the universe was created by the oneness force that you call God, but this god is not a singular god, it is an energy that is not split by gender. It is mother, it is father, it is the vastness of an energy that holds no tangible form. It is infinite love, complete joy, and perfect peace. When you reach God's door you reach infinite serenity. God does not punish, scare, or instill fear. God waits patiently while you learn from your mistakes, heal all soul wounds, create as a god, become God, and return back home as God.

Lemuria was pleasantly successful. Other star nations delegated with the Council of Light and received approval to join us. These other star nations were Sirius, Andromeda, Lyra, Orion, and later on, Bellatrix. Lemurians enjoyed their civilization and politely declined the genetic and technological advancements suggested by the Lyrans. (You will learn more about this in chapter 6.) To keep everyone happy, the Pleiadians started to work with the Lyrans on the creation of Atlantis. Lyra, Orion, and Bellatrix joyfully migrated to Atlantis and in unison, began to work on more futuristic projects.

During the time of Lemuria and Atlantis we had rejuvenation

temples and energy tools to keep our energy awake and vibrant so that we could move flexibly between dimensions. We had our full 5D consciousness, complete access to the Universal Mind, and direct contact with other life forces in the universe. We dreamt that Earth would become heaven in the universe, a place to visit and relax and enjoy oneself in the same way that you might go on a luxurious vacation to Hawaii, or visit an amusement park. Here your physical body would experience various thrills, as well as a full range of emotions, both good and bad. You would experience this roller coaster of emotions before going back home.

At this time, we were also determining how to find God, and hoping that while descending to the lower realms we would understand the soul's journey better. However, we misjudged it all. We found instead that when you lower your energy, you are limiting your consciousness and that without proper assistance you forget who you are. You wouldn't realize that the energies of Earth would put you on a roller coaster ride that never stops. When you enter the 3D realm it is as if you are in an altered state and you are apt to go into an induced sleeping mode.

INNER EARTH

Natural disasters are common on all planets and are part of the animate and inanimate evolution. We agreed not to interfere with the organic progression of Earth. There are several planets in the universe where life thrives in the inner parts of the planet versus the outside as it does on Earth as you know it today. For example, Maia in Pleiades is a volcanic planet and its surface is uninhabitable. In collaboration with other star nations we invented technology that allows the inner part of the planet to be a habitable and thriving environment for life. The volcanoes that exist there are our gateways into the inner parts. We have heat and fire-resistant materials that you have not discovered yet, which allow us to easily maneuver through hot masses.

We have used the same technology to create cities inside of the Earth beneath its surface and beneath deep bodies of water. Other star nations contributed to the inner Earth project, especially Sirius. After the Lemurian destruction many Sirians preferred to live in the cities within the Earth instead of on its surface. Later on in your history some parts of the inner Earth were used to protect human tribes from an extraterrestrial invasion known as the Battle for Earth until Earth was secured and freed of controlling gods (extraterrestrials who demanded sovereignty). Once this was accomplished the Council of Light established the Free Will Law, which granted Earth the right to evolve without external interference.

There is still thriving extraterrestrial life within your inner Earth for reasons of supporting your evolution. Some energy portals open to those with a pure heart and innocent intentions. We often advise you to be one with nature in the same way that you are one with the universe—for the purpose of connecting with the inner Earth. Many answers that you are seeking are right under your own nose.

ATLANTIS

Atlantis was the second extraterrestrial civilization on Earth to spring up as a sister community to Lemuria in order to satisfy other star nations' demands for a more technologically sophisticated community. Atlantis offered more freedom for us. In Lemuria, we were connected to our bodily senses, and natural elements of Earth. Physical manifestation and creation stemmed from merging these energies, rather than utilizing the sophisticated technology that was available to us. We were researching the potential of the energy from Earth's duality, as well as wanting to more deeply understand the way our soul and mind unified in the body. In Atlantis, many beings eventually abandoned organic ways of manifestation and living from the heart (feminine soul energy). Instead, they opted for the more sophisticated technology, that was already being used on other planets, that led them to live more dominantly from the mind (male intelligent energy).

While living in Atlantis, our extraterrestrial bodies showed signs of incompatibility with Earth's atmosphere, and started to experience disease to various degrees. Originally we had utilized plant DNA to modify our bodies. This enabled us to live in Earth's natural environment, yet at the same time we still had to frequently revisit our home planets to rejuvenate our energy. We also built several rejuvenation temples on Earth, but they were not enough to sustain all demands. Since the Earth is bound to the 3D energy, we had to utilize 3D bodies in order to be able to physically create anything here. This rule still applies today.

In Centaurus, Lyrans were already experimenting with DNA merging and genetic modifications, and suggested we use this technology on Earth to improve our 3D bodies. Further experiments in Earth's environment were needed and we all benevolently agreed to this, but we did not properly follow the time guidelines for these experiments and we utilized animal DNA. It was the closest to our kind, just extremely primitive. We wanted physical bodies that would function for longer periods of time while we enjoyed our stay on Earth.

With this in mind we advanced our extraterrestrial bodies, and consequently anchored our soul energy deep into the Earth. Later on in Atlantis and Sumer this technology was used without proper regulation and it got out of hand. The human psyche is fragile—but we came to realize that too late. By speeding up God's natural evolution by upgrading animals, merging animal and extraterrestrial DNA, opening them up to 4D and 5D energies without them really understanding who they were or how to utilize all the knowledge and energy, we had unintentionally plunged many innocent souls into mental insanity.

Originally it was agreed upon that no one would be allowed to alter Earth's evolution, but we all broke that agreement. Collectively we believed that we were making great advances toward our own evolution, but in fact our actions turned out to be a drawback for us all. It was much later that we realized that genetic DNA manipulation left huge scars on our souls.

For the most part, life in Atlantis was good until we realized that we had greatly overestimated the benefits of the animal DNA being used in the modification of our own physical bodies. A natural connection to the higher source was harder to keep and our minds became easily clouded and manipulated. We saw a split between those who had the highest intentions for Earth and were following the Law of One, and those who were just caught in the trap of the density of Earth's animalistic emotions such as greed, ego, jealousy, and a desire to dominate and control. These individuals were known as the Sons of Belial or, as we liked to call them, the ego-possessed beings.

Those who still held onto the integrity of the mission and stayed connected to their 5D selves foresaw the end of Atlantis long before it actually occurred. No one could stop the ego-possessed beings and prevent the disaster that would eventually manifest. We loved Earth, we loved our life in Atlantis, and we believed in the New Earth.

PRESERVING INFORMATION

Intuitively sensing the destruction of Atlantis, we began to preserve information on Earth to remind us of who we are and where we came from. We hid this information so it could be found by our future selves, which was something that we hadn't found necessary to do in Lemuria. We began to foresee that there was a great chance of disconnection between the 3D and 5D realms. Our intuition told us that it would be much easier to access information carefully hidden within the living Earth rather than train ourselves to connect with the 5D to access the Akashic Records or the Universal Mind.

The eyes are the windows of the soul. The heart is the seat of the soul. The star human is equipped with the intuition needed to discover all the clues we have hidden. Notice the combination of threes: your eyes (sixth chakra), your heart (fourth chakra), and your intuition (second chakra). Don't get confused, for it is the emotional feeling in each particular chakra (mentioned above) that activates your intuition, helps you to receive ancient knowledge through your heart, and allows your soul to see through your eyes. Your feelings are the key to unlocking your sleeping abilities.

The great task of saving humanity, with the intention of rescuing all the souls and showing them the way home, began. With great attention to details we created time capsules and programmed crystals, plants, trees, and bodies of water with light codes containing our energy and memories. The Earth became a library. This is exactly why you feel drawn to particular crystals, places on Earth, and spending time in nature, for instance. You hug trees, collect herbs, and create magnificent gardens. The light being within you unconsciously remembers the time when you walked on Earth in your 5D energy.

Ask to be led toward the stones and crystals that you have coded to find in the future. The future is now and you are ready to access your own energy. Put your bare feet and hands into the Earth and ask to be connected to the ancient knowledge that gave birth to wisdom. Ask questions and listen with your heart and your intuition for answers, before seeing with your eyes. The way home is in retracing your steps backward.

There were not enough of us to change the fate of Atlantis, but we knew that if we prepared and remained patient we could wait to enter another stellar activation cycle (a particular astrological time that allows the Earth realm to be more open to universal energies). This would mass awaken consciousness in those who were ready, and rescue those souls by teaching them who they truly are and showing them the path home. Several of these cycles have since passed but during this present time you are fortunate enough to be in one of these cycles again.

The 2012 stellar activation cycle opened time lines, your ancient memories, other realities, and access to parallel lives. You can now move consciously between the past, present, and future energies, although you have to be very careful not to get lost. The main purpose of looking into past energy is to heal your soul's PTSD, to release all emotional hurts, and bring healing. The healing will enlighten your soul, allowing you to become the writer of your future.

The destruction of Atlantis ripped open many dimensions, allowing low vibrational energies to gain access and attach themselves to living souls on Earth. We fought hard to close those dimensions and remove the parasitic energies that had gained entry. This resulted in closing access to the 4D and 5D in the physical body for all incoming souls. Everyone who would enter the reincarnation cycle, which eventually would apply to all of us, would have to cross the River of Forgetfulness without being allowed to use the Rainbow Bridge.

This resulted in forgetting who you were and how to get back home. The intention was to protect ourselves from self-destruction and soul suffering on Earth. At that time the Council of Light gave us a choice to leave the Earth forever and leave it as it was. They would induce a complete cleansing (wipeout) of all species living on and in the Earth, or we could stay, play gods, follow Earth's laws, and assist all those souls in the evolution without speeding up the process. Again, one of the tenets of Earth law is that what happens to a soul on Earth has to be healed on Earth. If a traumatic event was experienced in the physical body it has to be healed in the physical body. The catch is that the soul must be willing to be healed. This is the Free Will Law.

EGYPT

Many of us chose to stay. The Earth is an important part of the universe and its destruction would have had further consequences for all of us. We loved humans, for they were our children and we believed that everyone could change. Originally all souls came from the same source; there is just a difference in age. Each soul remembers its original essence, which is peace. On Earth the soul just takes on a personality and forgets its divine origin. Our divine work was to remind the soul that he or she is a part of the starseed family and that the human body is a part of the animal family.

There were several lineages that arrived from Atlantis. We will speak of the Egyptian lineage here, which was led by Master Thoth and followed by many various star beings living on Earth. Our souls were heavy in mourning after leaving Atlantis for it was our home, our love, and our sacred place.

Another lineage we will mention, as it is an important historical part of our past, was Sumer, which sprouted while Atlantis was still in its thriving stage. The majority of ego-possessed extraterrestrial beings migrated to Sumer and began to be known as gods.

After the destruction of Atlantis, the Council of the Light gave us new guidelines. We were allowed to teach anyone who was willing to learn about their celestial energy in moderation. This would allow for spiritual evolution without overwhelming the human psyche. Our intention was to rescue all the trapped souls and guide them home. The soul disconnection from Source presented many obstacles to our teaching. Spirituality, love, and light had to be embraced as a way of life instead of ego, lust, and the so-called easy materialistic life. Access to the Akashic Records and Universal Mind was still open. Those under the influence of the Sons of Belial viewed us as some kind of fanatics—crazy folks who'd lost their minds. Does that remind you of something from your life?

HONORING THE LAW OF FREE WILL

It hurt us not to be able to assist everyone at once. We learned to respect the wishes of others, even if we could clearly foresee destruction. We had our convictions to articulate and we showed our evidence, but we would not intimidate anyone into seeing things as we saw them. The soul has to choose its journey, whether it is happiness or suffering. To love someone unconditionally means to respect them and allow them to pick their own journey.

We encourage you to be a frequency holder of the highest available energy. We encourage you to embody the ambassador of your own star nation and represent your soul star family in the best possible way, and we ask you to respect the soul's wishes regarding those who are not yet ready to see the light. Offer choices and let them decide. Do not get frustrated and anxious because someone doesn't get it yet. Patience is one of the lessons we all have to learn.

MYSTERY SCHOOLS

We needed to build a new community to carry on our mission, and new headquarters for our star soul family. Egypt was already thriving with human slaves who were disconnected from Source. With remnants of our technology the pyramids, temples, and dwellings were gradually built in Egypt. The star beings thriving in the inner Earth assisted us and we interconnected many of our ancient structures with entrances to the inner cities. By this time the battle between dark and light had become public knowledge.

To preserve our ancient teaching for the future we embodied and documented history. We created mystery schools where students could gain full consciousness in the appropriate levels while transforming their ego. Today these lessons of the mystery schools are woven into your everyday life. We listen to you; we know you have no time to leave your family, or enough resources to seclude yourself into years of spiritual study. This is why, upon your awakening, you are challenged with tasks and transformations that are not always comfortable for you. Once you awaken from human hypnosis you enter the etheric mystery school. Some of you are conscious in your dreams and have memories of your studies. It is all real.

Many of you who are drawn to this message have lived in that time with us. You are us and we are you. Your soul remembers the times when you were an apprentice, healer, priestess, architect, or inventor. Your soul remembers the days you spent with your Atlantean tribe. Your soul also remembers the struggles and failures, the sadness and disappointment and the heartache—all of which manifest as blockages in current time. Your human energy wants to protect you from all those feelings so it is trying hard to prevent you from rekindling all the knowledge and ancient truths about yourself. The unconscious human mind just remembers the failure and feels ashamed and guilty, which induces infinite suffering if you allow it. The human is a scared animal who is programmed to survive and reproduce.

A starseed human is who you really are. You are a being of light living in a human body. You have a choice to find out more about yourself—about who you truly are.

ACCEPTANCE, FORGIVENESS, AND LOVE

It all starts with acceptance and forgiveness. Could you accept that you are an extraterrestrial being having a human experience? This could be the greatest shock of your life. Do not worry, you will not shape-shift into an odd-looking alien with bulging eyes. You will still be you on the outside, but you will allow for great changes within. The body is just a vessel that gets you from one hypnotic crazy lifetime into another. It is the soul within you that will wake from the long coma and the second shock wave will arrive right on schedule, with all the questions; what has happened to me? You may question; how could you have forgotten? How could you have agreed to so many lifetimes that brought you so much terrible suffering? Where were your guides? These are all great questions.

We know that forgiveness does not come easy in your realm, yet we encourage you to embark on a journey of forgiveness. When the answers start coming to you, when you learn who your star family is and where you belong, what your extraterrestrial skills are, what were your other lifetimes, who harmed you and who did you harm—always allow yourself to forgive others and forgive yourself. Holding grudges, being angry, or planning revenge does not serve you in any way. It lowers your vibration and holds you a prisoner. Practice a trinity of acceptance, forgiveness, and love that frees you from where you are right now.

And where were we all that time? Always by your side, but many times you were not willing to hear us. Sometimes we were your brothers and sisters, neighbors, or soul mates. We came into earth bodies the same way you came into yours and we found a way to free ourselves. Some are still there, creating pathways for all starseeds who are ready to go home. Remember the rule of the Earth body and physical creation. We can physically create only while in a physical body. We come to you and send you energy, love, and information. We witness your soul transformation and assist you every step of the way. Then it is up to you as to what you will do with your physical body. We cannot interfere in your life, but when you consciously invite us in, we can assist you on your journey.

NEW RULES

The Sumerian civilization was ended by the big flood. Once again, many of us were deeply invested in Earth's civilization, survival, and evolution. We delegated new rules that came from the Council of Light. We could not enter the Earth in our extraterrestrial body and interact visibly with humanity like we did. You used to call us gods and deities. Some extraterrestrial life such as fairies, mermaids, unicorns, and dragons, who survived on Earth, became a target for ego-possessed beings and had to retreat into the inner Earth or leave the Earth for good. We all could either incarnate in the human body or find someone who would become our prophet and communicate our words.

This rule would apply to all of us, Children of the Law of One and Sons of Belial alike. There have been some exceptions and broken rules, but for the most part we all followed the rules. The cities of the inner Earth had to be secured and forgotten about. Since the inner Earth is occupied by fifth-dimensional and higher-dimensional beings of light, they are all positive, have the highest intentions for humanity, and have to be kept secret until you are collectively in a higher vibration.

We would like to refresh your memory a little about incarnating in the human body after Sumer. During that time there were strong living communities whose energy and memories were fully open to the Lemurian and Atlantean lineages, teachings, and mastery that would allow them to live in 3D bodies with access to 5D knowledge and abilities. The rule of the human body was and still is that when you incarnate you cross the River of Forgetfulness and you forget who you were prior to that incarnation, not even remembering your lineage and ancestors. It is like being wiped clean when you enter the infant body. If you do manage to remember something, the first six years of your life will ensure that you forget it.

That is changing greatly right now. When you were born into an enlightened community you received appropriate assistance through energy work and teachings to help you remember your soul's origins and your extraterrestrial ancestors. Throughout your life you could master opening your energy to 5D energy and keeping the information living within you until you passed it on to other generations. Special importance was given to accessing the Akashic Records (the information about your soul journeys and experiences) and the Universal Mind (the intellectual information about the universe, its technology, and its inventions). The life span of your physical body was longer than you have in this current time.

A great example of a surviving Atlantean tribe was the Essene community, which involved the birth of Jesus Christ. Jesus Christ is a Pleiadian being and Mary Magdalene is a Sirian being. We understand this may upset you and cause a shock wave throughout your whole being. Jesus Christ and Mary Magdalene as well as many others in the Essene community demonstrated how, through energy work, spiritual discipline, and community support you all could master your own energy and be like them, because you *are* like them! You may have come from different star families, but the essence of a star being is the same—only your abilities may vary.

There have been twelve seeding races and each of them possesses special traits that are reflected in your own body as your unique skills. Some star nations mentioned below also served as portal door openers for others who might not be mentioned here.

Sirius * wisdom

Andromeda * healing

Pleiades * soul healing

Centaurus * the science of DNA

Epsilon Eridani * mediators and peacemakers

Lyra * watchers and ancestors

Arcturus * knowledge and healing

Pegasus * peacemakers and negotiators

Virgo * doctors, healers, and the medicine of the future

Orion, Bellatrix * knowledge, guardians, and protectors

Rigel, Mintaka * guardians and protectors

Alpha Aries * living art energy

We spoke of acceptance and forgiveness; the next step is love. Can you love yourself the way you are? Can you embrace yourself as perfect just the way you are? Can you love without judgment and need? Love heals. Love is stronger than death. Unconditional love for all Creation will illuminate your path back home.

We know that when you die on Earth and go to, as you call it, heaven to recount your experience you wonder why you were not able to figure out your full mission and heal all your soul traumas. The 4D of heaven is a tricky place. When you die here you are born out there, at the same second. As one family mourns the other celebrates. In heaven you have your memories, yet you are under the influence of the most beautiful, magnificent hypnotic energy. It is a great place, and all you have heard about it is true. However, this place is like a rejuvenation temple with the purpose of getting you excited to return back to Earth again with a heavy load of unhappy triggers so you can set yourself on a great journey of suffering so that one day, perhaps, you can remember who you are, what this is, and then die again without a chance of healing, thereby repeating the cycle.

What if you do not need to repeat the cycle? What if you have a choice to heal your soul and return home. How? You need to start to work with your conscious energy to release yourself from the time line of the past and the future. Heaven is 4D energy with a time line.

WORKING WITH CONSCIOUS ENERGY

Conscious energy is the energy of now, of the present time, of right now at this moment. It is not what happened in the past and it is not what will happen in the future. You need to slow down and stabilize yourself in the present moment. It is like stopping someone in their tracks and looking them straight in the eye.

The key to this ancient teaching is to awaken your consciousness in your physical body. When you feel drawn toward this information you will come to understand that everything happens for a reason. Sudden accidents and coincidences will no longer surprise you on your spiritual journey. Now you are consciously stepping into the teachings of your higher self and you are becoming your own teacher and guru. When you start utilizing your energy consciously, the shift you desire will happen much more quickly. You will start feeling better faster; you will see changes faster. You will no longer need to experience huge ups and downs.

Once you decide that you will remain in the present within your body instead of having your mind wander all over the place, your body may decide to give you a hard time because it fears the fact that you may now be in charge. The body's job is to ensure your survival and it usually does this by putting you in fearful situations or plunging you into chaos and then rescuing you. In this, it becomes your hero, making you feel that there is no one you can trust but yourself. Do you see the repetitive pattern?

When you are learning to hold yourself in the present time, again, you want to stabilize yourself in that energy. The best way to do this is to keep all your emotions neutral as much as you can. Your mind and body will challenge you, but if you manage to hold yourself in a neutral energy for a few days, everything will get easier. This is just the beginning. You will begin to see your life in a new light. You will learn to let go of bad thoughts from the past, and also not to overextend your energy into the future. This is a great exercise for you as a starseed to consciously start working with your energy and gradually master how to move between 3D, 4D, and 5D consciously, as you did in ancient times.

Your soul lives in your 3D body, but it cannot move to a higher dimension on its own; it needs your conscious help. Once it is connected with your higher self in 5D, you will learn how to bring that energy back into your physical body to enrich your everyday life, your work, and your life's purpose. It is the desire of your highest self that you be happy, have a joyful life, a wonderful family, and all that you need to thrive and be abundant. This could be you! Why not? As a lightworker, you came here with a mission. The universe does have your back and you can enjoy yourself while on Earth. You can have it all!

RESISTANCE

When you start to make conscious changes in your life, for example, shifting from a poor, sad, frustrating life pattern into an abundant, happy life pattern, your soul might experience a temporary shock from such a change. It can cause temporary chaos and resistance because a change is intimidating to the human body. Change is like walking over a shaky old bridge; it can be frightening.

The first half of the struggle is to confidently step over the missing planks and prove to yourself that you really want it, that you can do this. You may fall a few times, but that does not scare you. You then reach the middle part, and the bridge is now easier to walk on because of what you learned while struggling with the first half. Then when you are about two-thirds of the way to reaching your goal, you will start to doubt yourself. Could this really be so easy? Is there a trap on the other side? And suddenly you notice all the missing planks again and you become afraid of falling and ultimate failure and you resist taking another step. If you do not reach the end of the bridge you do not accomplish your goal.

All you need to do is stabilize yourself by staying in the neutral energy of your emotions. Feel neither excitement of changing nor fear of possible failure. Review what you have achieved so far. Are your goals still the same or do they need some re-adjustment? Believe in yourself and you will succeed.

Resistance is just a form of fear.

Layers of resistance exist in the upper layers of your aura. They are like a rubbery, bouncy material that literally keeps bouncing you back from achieving your goals. The way to break through this resistance is to have fire in the soul. The fire is like your fuel. Turn your fears into fire and walk over that shaky bridge with fire in your soul.

CONTACT

The most common question we hear is, When will we land our spaceships on Earth? The best answer we can give you is that we are already here. All starseeds on Earth are ambassadors of their star nation. You are the extraterrestrial beings living on Earth in human form, which is how we lived there eons ago. Some of you are our children, some of you are children of other star nations, and some of you are us. The blockage you have is that you do not believe that you have full consciousness to access the ancient wisdom, inventions, technologies, and knowledge we had. You think you need some special upgrade of your human body to be like we were when we roamed the Earth. You already are like us. The special light codes you are seeking to activate are hidden within you and are activated by the frequency of love. Once you learn to hold the frequency of love within, you will have access to all you seek. Could it be that easy? Yes, it is.

Love is the essence of everything. Love is the universal energy that your soul has never forgotten; it connects you to your star home. Through all the incarnations when the alien within you became more human and you eventually experienced soul trauma, accepted programs of fear and control, fell into a deep spiritual coma, and were trapped in the incarnation cycle, there remained one energy that you have never been able to completely forget. It is the energy that may present the most blockages and fears for you. It is the energy of *love,* which creates a better tomorrow.

Many of you have seen spaceships in the sky and perhaps you've had a personal UFO encounter. There are many of us surrounding the Earth and holding the higher available frequency for the best outcome of future events. We cannot interfere with your physical life, for example your governments, as you would like us to do. It would be against the universal law, which we all must obey. Free Will Law on Earth is part of the Universal Law. Unless there is 100 percent agreement among Earth beings that we should interfere with your chain of events, we cannot come and give our assistance as regards physical changes of your world and its events, whether they are positive or negative. We love you and it emotionally hurts us to witness you suffer, yet we respect your collective decisions and keep our distance.

Now, there is a clue in your Free Will Law. Think about it: even bad things in your world originate from the Free Will Law. The ego-possessed beings know how to trick you. They know how to dangle nice shiny objects under your nose, how to give you a false helping hand during the most difficult times of your life so you can sign away your life to them. You willingly become a slave of society because you believe it is something you have to do. This persists until you wake up from all those false beliefs and find yourself trapped in heavy chains, under their control, living in fear, and believing there is no way out.

Love is the way out.

Free Will Law works on the collective level, but also on individual level. Just as you agree to accept all levels of karma, you can also renounce your karma, your vows, and your promises. This is as simple as opening a new door and saying goodbye to your past. The trick is, first, to consciously understand the totality of your past, forgive others and yourself for what happened, and then walk through a new door and into a world without your old karma, with no trace of guilt, shame, or fear. You can do this.

You can also call upon your soul family to assist you in your life. Just because we cannot land in your backyard and have a picnic with you does not mean we cannot make a personal connection with you. When you freely state that you wish to connect with us, we can temporarily bring you aboard our spaceship. Most often we do this when you are sleeping and then return you to your body so you can go about your daily life.

The most precious gift we can give you is to awaken you from your hypnotic sleep. When you accept that there is more to life than what you are living, we will empower you in your transformation and shower you with clues to hidden knowledge so you will ultimately become the creator of your own future. Metaphorically speaking, we are shining a light on your path, but according to Free Will Law it is you who must walk that path. You have a choice. You always have, you just forgot this. Just as we wish to assist you in embodying the highest vibration, other beings have an interest in keeping you at the lowest vibration in order to enslave you. Their souls are also incarnating on Earth to make negative changes to your planet.

Then there are souls we connect with who channel us. The best channelers we choose are the starseeds of our home planet because they remember our energy imprint. Always discern the messages you are hearing. Listen to all of the messages with your heart, not with your mind. If the message touches your heart and it leaves you uplifted and hopeful about your future, it is a message from higher vibrational beings. Channeled messages should not instill any fear or despair within you; it should not flame your ego or give you orders. Remember your free will. You have a choice as to what actions you will take. You have the ultimate choice to do good or evil.

We the Pleiadians are connecting with you from the past and also from the future. Again, those from the past have left many clues for you to learn about who you are and what your home planet is so that you may liberate yourself and embrace the freedom you deserve.

The past is solidified, but the future is variable and it is up to you what future we all will have. Everything depends on your current actions. We have a great interest in assisting you. The human body is a gift, for the human body can make physical changes in the Earth realm. We would like you to embrace your star origins and ask yourself questions like, What changes does the Earth need? What does humanity need? How can I be of service?

If you would ask us, we think that humanity needs to embrace love, compassion, and kindness for one another. We hear you, that you would like to move to another planet; that you are done with life on Earth and that you suffer so much. But what did you learn? You are still separating yourself by race, color, language, and social status. You feel betrayed by us and by God. But will you believe us when we tell you that since the days of Atlantis we have been offering assistance to you, trying to help you find your way out of the incarnational cycle? The only way you can leave your Earth for good is to end your incarnational cycle by liberating yourself and finding your way back home. You can do this as an individual or with your soul family. When you do this you leave a trail of energy for others to follow.

We, the Pleiadians, are soul healers. We give you knowledge. Knowledge is a power that has to be used wisely. It is your birthright to make choices in your life! Use the knowledge to make the right choices and use love to heal all of your soul wounds.

Embrace being different! We love you unconditionally.

THE PLEIADIANS

1

Andromeda

Y ou can find the Andromeda constellation in the Northern sky. Andromedans celebrate diversity in their home world, as it is a nation of Andromedans, Pleiadians, Sirians, and Lyrans. Andromeda is also the primary home world to intelligent Silver Dolphins that live in vast oceans within this universe. Silver Dolphins are equal to any other beings on Andromeda. Their particular appearance and the fact that they live underwater does not set them apart.

THE ANDROMEDAN BEINGS

Andromedans are "Beings of Light" who are dedicated to bringing new technologies and holistic forms of healing to the entire universe, and they strive to assist other star nations to live in peace and unity.

Andromedans have been incarnating on Earth since the time of ancient Atlantis. Together with various star nations they cocreated new human life and repopulated the Earth. Interestingly, they created new souls on Earth who had not yet experienced universal life. During psychic readings, I have connected with several starseeds whose soul journey started in Atlantis (where their soul life was created). These souls are known as Atlantean Earth seeds. These Atlantean Earth seeds have one thing in common: they have a deeper connection to the Earth than those whose soul journey started in the universe prior to coming to live on Earth. Even though their soul was "first born" on Earth, they are still considered starseeds. They carry their ancestral parents' DNA (depending on where their ancestors came from, which typically is Andromeda or Pleiades). The only difference is that they do not have their own soul memories of these planets, only energy imprints from their parents.

Andromedans lived peacefully in ancient Atlantis with other star people. Some remembered consciously where they came from and some forgot, because of the 3D density of the Earth world. Together with others, they learned, shared their own knowledge, and strived to create an amazing world. In the end, those of the light and higher vibrations could not prevent the end of Atlantis. Despite losing their dreamland, they were able to preserve all of the teachings by "planting the seeds," especially their knowledge, within crystals. Many "light codes" were thus placed in various crystals and in the living body of water to assist future generations.

Andromedan starseeds are mysteriously drawn to Atlantean Earth seeds, even on an unconscious level. This connection helps them awaken their memory and their abilities, and it gives them a sense of their mission.

You can meet Andromedans with pure, single DNA and those with combined, merged DNA. Under the Lyrans' guidance they merged their DNA with other star nations to create beings who would be empowered on their mission through the universe.

There are many possibilities in DNA merging. One combination I often see is the Andromedan/Pleiadian types, who are especially gifted healers. The other type is Adromedan/Sirian and sometimes Lyran (the fathers and mothers of the DNA merging process). Beings with this type of DNA have gifts of healing, but their healing knowledge is more connected and focused toward science, research, development, and bioengineering. It is quite common for Andromedan/Sirian starseeds to have at least two guides, each from their own star system, their soul family. Andromedan guides usually focus on healing and Sirian guides will bring their knowledge, wisdom, and intellect to them. In so doing, Sirian guides provide opportunities to learn and progress. Each guide will bring their own wisdom and energy to the situation and assist in developing abilities that are unique to their home world.

Andromedans are clever in many areas, although Andromedan healers of the physical body and scientists stand out the most. It is not just a coincidence that so many are incarnating on Earth at this time to assist humanity.

THE HOME WORLD

The Andromedan star system is a combination of dry land, trees, and a vast body of water. The land has colorful trees that are orange, purple, and brown. Their home on the land is very similar to the homes found on Sirius and the Pleiades. When journeying to Andromeda, I always sense that water covers most of the land. I am reminded about the deep-water connection of Andromedan starseeds. Understanding water, its energy, power, and flow, helps them in developing their own special abilities.

On many of my astral travels I have been guided into Andromeda's underwater world. When you astral travel, it does not matter if you have the ability to breathe underwater or not. On the astral plane you can breathe and see in the same way that you can on Earth. The enchanted underwater world glows in hues of all shades of blue. These colors are so rich and magnificent. If you wonder how the water tastes (salty or sweet), you will be surprised to discover that your taste buds turn into "feel buds," and instead of tasting water, you will sense the water with your whole being.

Andromeda's underwater world is full of exotic flowers and living creatures that are hard to describe, as the words for them are not in our vocabulary. This is a home of the Silver Dolphins. Silver Dolphins have a silver, sparkly glow around them. The presence of these majestic intelligent beings feels magical and angelic on all levels.

In addition to being able to taste with your whole being, this underwater world teaches you to feel energy through your whole being, using your "feeling" sensors or clairsentience as we call it. You learn to become one with the water and with the beings living there. Once you get used to the clairsentient sensations in your body and let this energy flow through you, you will easily learn to become one with the element of the water. Then you can continue to journey to this home world, observe its beauty, its marvels, and its magic with your eyes and mind. You may understand this on your first visit, or you could be journeying to this place many times before you learn to put your thinking mind aside and enjoy the experience. After mastering the basic sensing skills, you are able to view more of this world, which is comparable to swimming lessons in our world. You cannot swim in deep water until you have mastered these swimming skills.

When on an underwater journey into Andromeda, you will meet many exotic beings. Majestic seahorses are one such being, which by our vocabulary and understanding have only been described in fairy tales. The seahorses swim around and assist you in getting where you need to go. The other beings to mention are golden illuminated starfish emanating brilliant golden light energy that surrounds you when you are in their energy field. Their energy is serene and helps you to eliminate any pain (physical or emotional) you may experience at this time.

The starfishes' peaceful energy calms down all new nervous visitors who astral travel here (consciously or unconsciously). On these astral visits, Andromedan and Atlantean starseeds are able to connect their home world to their original soul energy. These astral journeys are an important part in soul awakening and assist in activating DNA.

After a refreshing relaxation in a starfish's golden light, you may notice silver sparkling light penetrating the water, resembling sunrays. The silver light is the energy emanating from the Silver Dolphins. When silver light combines with your energy, you may experience a beautiful tingling sensation in your hands and your whole body. To be in the presence of Silver Dolphins feels like angels are surrounding you. When their loving and healing energy merges with your whole being, you may feel like a beautiful mermaid/merman. This place is truly an underwater heaven and its energy is highly seductive.

Andromedans built huge caves in their underwater world. These caves serve as meeting places for Andromedans and other star nation members. Ceremonies, meditations, celebrations, planning, and schooling take place in these underwater caves.

ENERGY POWER CENTER (EPC)

Each star nation has its own signature abilities. In our human body, we have what I call an Energy Power Center (EPC). This energy power center connects to your strongest ability, depending on your DNA. This is the place where you receive energy information and process it. You also emanate and vibrate energy out of this center. This EPC may be located in a particular chakra, or may be two or more chakras merged; it depends on your DNA. If you have single DNA, you have one EPC. If you have merged DNA, you have two or more EPCs.

An Andromedan's EPC is in their third chakra; clairsentience is their strongest natural ability. When they first start to notice their abilities, Andromedan starseeds experience discomfort in their stomach. This odd feeling is from energy waves traveling through their bodies. They may feel confused about why they mostly feel energy in their body but cannot see the energy with their inner eye or receive telepathic communication. For Andromedans the clairsentient energy waves in the body are their natural way of perceiving energy, and they need to learn its meaning. After they learn to understand that this energy has its own language they very easily move to master other abilities such as telepathy, clairaudience, clairvoyance, and more.

ANDROMEDAN STARSEEDS ON EARTH

Andromedan starseeds are strongly connected to nature. They are attracted to water, especially the body of the ocean. They have an unexplainable love of dolphins and other animals. Dolphins and water bring their soul comfort, as this energy reminds them of their home world.

They are creative beings. They love different colors and like to combine them together without even consciously knowing why. Andromeda is full of various colors and their souls remember it. For example, they would not decorate a room in one shade. Instead they would bring many different colors together to create a nice, warm, nurturing effect. This skill makes them very tasteful decorators. In metal, they usually prefer silver over any other metal. All Andromedans that I have met are very gifted healers of the physical body.

As mentioned before, Andromedan starseeds may have single Andromedan DNA or merged DNA with other star nations. Those with single Andromedan DNA who I have worked with tend to have one thing in common: a back injury. It is interesting to note that the majority of these Andromedans have been in a car accident or some other kind of accident. After much observation, I have concluded that this injury awakened their natural ability; it was their triggering point.

Some have had miraculous recoveries from very bad accidents when doctors predicted that they would never walk again, but they fully recovered while others took longer to heal. All whom I have met who had physical health challenges were drawn to energy-healing modalities such as hands-on healing, and most of them became healers. In my experience, an awakening point for Andromedan starseeds comes with physical injury or a challenging illness. This pattern seems to apply mostly to those with single Andromedan DNA. Those with merged DNA may experience the same or a different kind of awakening.

In addition, I would like to point out that if you consciously work on your spiritual growth, you may avoid many unpleasant triggering points you agreed to prior to your incarnation. You may wonder, why did I have this car accident (for example)? What is this physical illness about? The answer is simple. If you run out of options from Western medicine, for instance if you are told that there is no cure for your illness, or that you need to learn to live with your physical condition for the rest of your life, then you might look into other possibilities that you may not have considered before. Your physical challenges may bring you to a totally different path than the one you've anticipated being on.

There have been many Andromedan starseeds who came to me out of frustration because they cannot see energy and wish that their third eye would open. Some of them have been trying to achieve this ability for a very, very long time. The answer is simple. They are focusing on the wrong ability to develop. They do have clairvoyant abilities, but they will not become strong until they learn about their primary ability to sense energy through their body, starting in the solar plexus.

An Andromedan's gift is to have what I call a "liquidy" energy that is part of their being. It is immensely important for Andromedan starseeds in their current lifetime to acknowledge this liquidy energy and connection with water. Once they understand their energy, their spiritual growth comes quickly.

The best way to describe their liquidy energy is to imagine a quiet water surface and a droplet of water falling down on it in slow motion. When the droplet hits the water, the surface ripples powerfully in all directions. Now imagine that instead of seeing the ripples with your eyes, you just feel the vibrations of the ripples in your body. This is how Andromedans perceive energy: as vibrations through their body.

The Andromedan rule is that you don't need to see or hear if you can feel!

The same applies to receiving messages and guidance until they learn to interpret the energy language without any words given to them. Instead of receiving energy messages telepathically, Andromedans receive messages in the form of energy waves, or feelings that pass through their third chakra and then throughout their bodies. It is crucial to their spiritual development to learn to interpret this energy language and learn to use their whole body as one "sensing machine." After that their third eye and other abilities can open. The reason for this is because if they are allowed to see or hear clearly before learning to interpret energy vibrations in their body, finding words for it and its meaning, it would become too easy for them and they would become easily disconnected. They would not strive to work hard or learn to understand the healing energy that flows through their bodies.

Andromedans must be one with this energy to be effective healers. I compare this spiritual progression to a baby trying to walk before learning to stand up and hold its balance. You have to take one step at a time. Please note this is a unique spiritual pathway for Andromedans; it varies for other star nations.

Once Andromedans learn how to work with their EPC (third chakra), the rest of their work becomes much easier. While passing their hands over a client during an energy-healing session, they can read the energy vibrations in their own body. (I call this a human X-ray.) By so doing they can intuitively diagnose any issue. They are literally a living, scanning, energy machine—if you want to look at it that way.

Andromedans are natural empaths and it is important that they release all the energy imprints they've collected throughout the day from their bodies. This should be done at least once a day; a good energy cleansing routine is very important!

Andromedans are passionate about classical music. When carrying out a reading for an Andromedan starseed client, I heard in my inner ear the Andrea Bocelli song "Con te Partiro." My client confirmed that she loves classical music and that it always raises her vibration. Many starseeds resonate with classical music. I would like to point out the connection between Andromedans and Andrea Bocelli. Andromedans are *amazing* healers, especially where physical illness is concerned. They do not need eyes to see, just like Mr. Bocelli. They *feel* energy vibrations throughout their wonderful beings. They can work with their eyes shut and produce incredible miraculous healings.

All you need to do, Andromedan starseeds, is to close your eyes and let your light shine completely. Listen to what your body vibrations are telling you and follow their lead. It may seem scary at first to follow "water wave-like vibrations," but you will be amazed at what you are capable of accomplishing and the healing you will both undergo and be able to do!

PRACTICES FOR ANDROMEDAN STARSEEDS

+ **When meditating, using any recordings that feature ocean or water sounds** to evoke the Andromedan atmosphere is extremely helpful. They are calming and soothing, helping to reduce stress as well as recharge your energy. While meditating, ask the element of water to awaken the light codes of your ancient memories within you.

+ **Visiting the beach, nature, and walking barefoot** can revive your energy. When you surround yourself with the natural environment, you're allowing your body to relax and your mind to clear. You can shift away from the day's routine to focus on the sights and sounds around you, like the rustle of tree leaves, or waves gently coming ashore. Your energy field will be enriched by the vibrational frequencies of trees and plants, green spaces, water, and the resonance of the Earth. Walking barefoot (called earthing or grounding) has great health benefits, like reducing inflammation and improving sleep, so kick off your shoes when possible and deepen your connection to the natural world.

+ **Listening to the sounds of dolphins and nature** has a profound impact on well-being. Research shows these sounds have a host of health benefits, such as the ability to boost mood and influence immune function. Play nature sounds as background music for increased harmony and a relaxed state of mind. Listen to these sounds with your whole body and pay attention to how they make you feel, instead of just listening with your ears. Soon you will be inspired to begin training your Andromedan clairsentience ability

+ **A regular energy cleansing routine, especially with water,** is essential for Andromedan starseeds to assist you in releasing and cleansing negative energy and imprints from other people's illnesses or problems you may have empathically sponged in. Develop a routine that is easy to do, such as soaking in a bath with essential oils and sea salt. An energy cleansing bath is a ritual that releases negative vibrations and harmonizes your physical and spiritual energies. Use visualizations to bring in fresh energy, sweep away energetic debris, and create a strong aura that glows with vitality. And when taking a shower, imagine the water as fresh, supercharged energy. It clears and heals as it flows over you, with unwanted energies swirling down the drain. After clearing your field, visualize divine energy filling your aura with insight and joy.

+ **Working with "human pendulum" energy** using the following exercise is beneficial as well.

ENERGY EXERCISE
✳ Become a Pendulum ✳

Quiet your mind and open your energy. Imagine your chakras are filled with the essence and color of each particular chakra, one by one, starting at your feet and continuing upward until this energy flows out of your crown chakra.

Focus on your stomach area. Notice your breath coming in and out. Tune in with your body. Listen to your body from inside. As you breathe in and out and tune in to your body, you will become more aware of your own energy.

Now you will ask simple yes and no questions and will pay attention to the subtle energy in your own body, noting how it reacts to each question.

Ask obvious yes answer questions such as, Is my name . . . [use your name]? so you can receive a positive yes answer. Now consciously notice the energy movement in your body. It may go up or down, or sideways; you should be able to sense some energy movement. This is your yes answer.

Repeat the same exercise with a question that will have no as an obvious answer. For example, asking whether you are a woman when you are a man. When you consciously receive your no answer, the energy will move in the other direction in your body or you will feel nothing.

Now you have the basic yes/no communication with the energy you are receiving or channeling. You can use this skill in your everyday life.

At the end, close your energy by pulling your chakras' colors in.

✳ ✳ ✳

Learning to open and close to energy to protect your energy field is essential for any starseed with heightened empathy. Think about your energy boundary. Is it open, closed, or just partially open? We open our energy field to let others in, to receive information, and to access divine energy. Closing our field protects us in situations where we don't want to absorb negativity. Selectively permitting some access to our field is accomplished when we set specific intentions, choosing what to allow in and what to exclude.

These practices are suitable for any starseed. Practice finding your energy boundary by bringing your attention first to your body, then to the energy that extends outside it. Sometimes that field is only inches from your body, and at other times it can extend several feet from it. With practice you'll become aware of your field, and can decide upon the right level of access or protection to use in different circumstances.

1-2-3 MINI-EXERCISE
✳ Open and Close to the Energy ✳

Open

Have an intention to open/widen your energy field so you can be connected to your guides.

Have a personal prayer, word, or symbol that becomes your activation code to open your chakras

Switch on your light in your seven chakras (metaphorically) to extend your energy field and your perception.

Close

Have an intention to close your energy.

Express your gratitude to those who've assisted you, and to yourself.

Switch off your light in your seven chakras (metaphorically) to make your energy field smaller, and tight like a protective cocoon around your body.

2

The Pleiades

The Pleiades, also known as the Seven Sisters, is a star cluster located in the constellation of Taurus. It is home to various star nations and extraterrestrials, including amphibian and dinosaurian beings. It is also home to the Lyrans, who settled peacefully in this constellation after the destruction of their world. Pleiades is a soul-healing station with visitors from other star nations who go there to study, relax, and heal.

The home worlds of the Pleiadians are breathtaking; this is my soul's home. As a child, when I would close my eyes, I would see magnificent rays of colors merged together, comparable to those of a kaleidoscope. I felt the love! I didn't know this was how my soul family communicated with me. I just felt comfort and love and I thought everyone could feel like that. I thought everyone had an imaginary world they could escape into.

THE PLEIADIAN BEINGS

Just like many other beings from various star nations, Pleiadians are extremely spiritually developed. Their bodies are composed of light energy, therefore a physical body is not required, but some prefer to have it. They are interested in helping us, the Earth humans, to evolve to a higher dimension. Pleiadians have been assisting us from the time of Earth's creation since they participated in seeding it. Many have chosen

36

to incarnate at this time to assist with the current changes. Pleiadian beings connect with Earth telepathically through various channelers. Currently they are reaching out to us from the future in an effort to assist with the creation of the New Earth.

Pleiadians are beings of Light and their mission is to teach us to embrace Love and Light as an evolving pattern. They are gifted soul healers and have the ability to connect with a soul, view its past or future, and deliver healing on a soul level. Pleiadian starseeds are Warriors of Light who came to Earth to assist in the awakening and evolving processes. Their mission is to help you remember who you are, what your unique abilities are, and what your life's purpose is. Pleiadians also have a close bond with Andromedans and Sirians. They participate in many ceremonial events and work in harmony with other star nations.

THE HOME WORLD

The Pleiadian star cluster is also known as the Seven Sisters. It has several planetary bodies, but seven of them are directly connected through mythology to Earth's creation story. An Earth week has seven days, Earth has seven continents, and the human body has seven main chakras that are essential in creating a rainbow body for the purpose of ascension. The seven celestial bodies in Pleiades represent the seven Pleiadian Cosmic Mothers, each a little different than the other. Many of you have lived in the Pleiades, and the Cosmic Mothers have lived on Earth.

Atlas
Atlas, one of the Seven Sisters, is a star in the Pleiadian constellation known for its vast oceans. It is home to intelligent Silver Dolphins from the Andromedan star system. Many water creatures living on Atlas are unknown to us on Earth. The sky colors on Atlas vary from pastel hues to bright orange, red, and pink. This is a great place for those wanting to learn the art of healing, perhaps with the Andromedan dolphins. Here you can learn to become one with the element of water and perceive information through your feeling center instead of through telepathy.

Electra

Electra, another star of the Pleiadian constellation, is a sacred healing place with much of its land covered by incredibly huge tall trees. The trees serve as healing chambers; they contain sacred and intelligent energy offering wisdom and ancient truths. The trees have been native to Electra for thousands of years and are comparable, for example, to mature oak trees. The color of these enormous trees ranges from dark brown, deep blue, dark purple, to deep green. The trunk is brown in color and the texture of the bark is similar to what we are familiar with on Earth. The trees' crowns are rich with branches full of healthy leaves. Some leaves are easily reachable by hand; others are so high they can barely be seen by the naked eye. Noticeably there are no fallen branches or leaves on the ground. The trees create very dense surroundings and when standing next to them it is difficult to view the sky above. Plucking of the leaves from the branches is considered disrespectful.

Upon entering Electra you will receive a guardian who will show you around. Pleiadian starseeds that connect to Electra will also have their guardian serve as a guide during their Earth life. Temporary guardians may also be chosen based on your energy needs. The guardian will escort you to the appropriate tree to fit your needs. You will then teleport inside the tree into the healing chamber. There you will become one with the tree and experience absolute unity. There are no doors or windows, yet the atmosphere inside the tree is serene. The green forest trees are extraordinary in energy and allow only light healers to go inside them.

My Experience Visiting Electra

I experienced visiting Electra and the sacred trees when soul traveling with a client. While describing what I saw, my client was able to recall memories of being there. She finally understood her love and obsession for trees and their energy. Electra is her home planet and her Pleiadian name is Seje.

During another soul journey to Electra with Seje, she had the privilege to go inside a special green tree. Our guardian communicated that

Seje needed the energy of this tree to heal and rejuvenate. When teleporting inside, it appeared as if she was swallowed by the tree. Although not invited to visit this tree, the energy I experienced on the outside was an energy of deep serenity. Afterward I was offered a tree to visit; it was a beautiful deep blue and instantly I cherished its energy. Once inside, a sense of peace and weightlessness came over me. I was one with the tree's energy! An incredible release of energy and feelings of comfort permeated me and my immediate environment. The energy became so intense and beautiful that there were simply no words to describe the experience. I felt as though I was wrapped in a deep blue fog and it felt incredibly good; my body had no weight and my soul soared with joy!

The healing energy of the tree was stunning, and I wondered if Seje was experiencing something similar. We communicated telepathically with our guide; he communicated that Seje would also need to visit an orange tree. There was only one orange tree, and there was a long line to enter it. Seje walked out of the green tree smiling and feeling happy, with a nice, slightly different energy about her. Even though she was supposed to go into the orange tree, she felt ready to teleport to the Sirius star system, where we were greeted by her soul mate.

Maia

Maia, another amazing star of the Seven Sisters in the Pleiades constellation, has many volcanoes on its surface and a huge portion of it is covered by water. When journeying to Maia you will see darkness as there is no sunlight at all. When experiencing this for the first time, I was puzzled. My guides shared with me that because of many active volcanoes, the surface of Maia is uninhabitable and the ashes from the volcanoes have created dark clouds; thus my perception of darkness. The volcano is a tunnel into the underworld and can be entered whether it is active or not. Pleiadians have developed the technology to live in the center of this planet.

The inner world of Maia is breathtaking and very similar to our life on Earth, with many plants and trees. I am reminded of the Crystal Cities that are in the inner Earth. If you teleported into one such city you wouldn't know that you were under the planet's surface. Seeing sunlight, blue sky, and signs of life is perfectly normal there. I often wondered how this was achieved. My guides showed me huge panels comparable to solar panels and explained that Maias use heat from the volcanoes or from the core of the planet to generate energy that is transmuted into natural light, heat, and electricity. In addition, the majority of Maia's cities are built under the water's surface and use the element of water for their living benefit.

Maia's Pleiadian starseeds are a little different from their Pleiadian brothers and sisters. All starseeds from Maia that I have channeled have an interesting connection or fascination with volcanoes, volcanic rocks, fire, and heat. These starseeds have an ability to absorb high temperatures without being bothered by them. Once they realize their home-world abilities, they can close their chakras in and keep a cooling layer of the energy around them, even in the extreme heat. I suppose many firefighters on Earth came from Maia! These starseeds also have a special connection to sound healing, music, and musical composition. Living in the inner planet helped them to fine-tune the listening capabilities of their inner ear and their ability to perceive sound.

Alcyone

Alcyone is the brightest star in the Pleiades cluster. The Pleiadians consider it their sacred "soul retreat planet," and the energy on it is deeply spiritual. The main Pleiadian Healing Temple of Love and Light is located in the mountain on Alcyone. This is a sacred place and only those with higher energy vibrations are allowed to visit it. Personally, I view Alcyone as the most special place in the whole universe and consider it my home.

Several things stand out on Alcyone. First is its energy. When you land on this beautiful planet the first thing you notice is its liquid-like energy of light, which feels like poured honey, thick in consistency, but lovely and without the stickiness. As soon as you enter, this liquid energy wraps around you and your energy field. Second, the air is a little dense for Earth humans to breathe.

Covered with mountains and bodies of water, Alcyone is abundant, with various trees and flowers. There are many exotic birds and animals too difficult to describe with our vocabulary. There are also buildings made from glass-like material, which have a futuristic appearance.

The skies of Alcyone are full of colorful clouds made of liquid light energies that gently move and sway with the breeze. The colors of this liquid light energy are similar to Arctic lights, ranging from all the shades found in a rainbow to other vibrant colors beyond description. When consciously observing and absorbing the sky of Alcyone with your own eyes and in your whole being, your soul, you will fully grasp the meaning to the expression *the eyes are the window to the soul.* The color of the sky has a soothing effect and brings serenity, harmony, and peace. This could be why the structures built on Alcyone are made of glass-like material: it allows this incredible energy to filter through.

Here you will also meet various members of other star nations, all of whom have harmonious vibrations and choose to live or visit Pleiades. Many star brothers and sisters visit this wonderful place for soul healing and/or soul growth.

Healing Journey to Alcyone's Pleiadian Healing Temple

During a healing journey with Kai-Hi, my client and a Pleiadian starseed, we traveled to Alcyone's Pleiadian Healing Temple. The temple, which appears to be made of stone, is a tall steep structure built in a triangular shape and of a deep blue color. At the bottom of the temple is a staircase that leads one up and inside. The healing temple can be accessed in one of two ways. The first way is by using this staircase and the second way is by teleporting visitors in. Both cases require the "proper clearance"—usually an invisible symbol in the Language of Light that is hidden in the palm of their hand. Taking the staircase is more beneficial for the soul, as it will adjust the energy level of the visitor, and help with a conscious remembering of the journey while taking one step at a time.

Kai-Hi and I were standing at the bottom of the temple before our slow ascent up the staircase. While climbing up, we noticed a blue "fog" surrounding our feet. Eventually, this fog-like energy surrounded our entire bodies. This was such an amazing and beautiful experience; our chakra centers filled up with the blue Pleiadian energy! We became overwhelmed with a sense of knowing that we belonged here, for we both have a Pleiadian soul. In time we reached the gate and were greeted by Pleiadian beings known as the Gate Watchers. Dressed in white robes tied at the waistline with blue twisted belts, these Gate Watchers reminded us of monks. When greeting Kai-Hi, she felt their love and sensed that they recognized her. They asked us to place our palms up and they placed theirs over ours, reading the light symbols in our palms (or our energy—if you do not have a symbol). Next we were guided to touch the gate and it began to open.

Kai-Hi felt that she remembered the inside of the temple. We strolled past oversize baths carved into the ground that were filled with liquid energy; in them one could rest, heal, and rejuvenate the soul. Kai-Hi was instructed that as a Pleiadian light healer she would be allowed to bring and guide her clients into this healing temple during sessions and upon her invitation. In the middle of the temple is a very special place: an octagon-shaped energy vortex that I have visited many times. Kai-Hi was anxious to explore this place, as her next step was to work with this energy vortex in her Earth life. This is where conferences and "Council of Light" meetings take place.

At this time the guide asked Kai-Hi to sit in the center of the octagon. As soon as she sat down, healers from other star systems, including Arcturians, Andromedans, Sirians, Centaurians, Lyrans, Pleiadians, Pegasian beings, and healers from Virgo, started to teleport in. Kai-Hi was sitting in the center of the octagon formation while these healers extended their energy toward her, attuning her with their energy. Now she is able to use their signature energy in her work with clients as part of her Earth life mission.

ENERGY POWER CENTER (EPC)

Pleiadians are soul healers. Their Energy Power Center is located in the fourth chakra, the "heart chakra." Pleiadians receive, perceive, sense, and send energy through their heart and soul. When ready to engage in energy healing, their heart center will increase in size and color, which indicates that their EPC is activated and ready for use. This heart energy feels like an explosion of brilliant energy between the third and fifth chakras. This energy ring is usually viewed as a blue, green, pink, or golden color. The heart/soul energy is a Pleiadian's strongest energy, thus it should be used consciously as the central focus of all of the work and healing they do.

PLEIADIAN STARSEEDS ON EARTH

Pleiadian starseeds have incarnated on Earth for many lifetimes and have served as lightworkers in their previous lives. Pleiadian starseeds are gentle souls who emanate an energy of pure love. These souls thrive on love; they need to feel loved, and they give their love freely. They are the seeds of love! Pleiadian starseeds are very honest and sincere, and they do not intentionally lie, cheat, or take advantage of others. They are natural givers with a strong tendency to put others before themselves, which often results in a "burned-out" feeling.

Pleiadian starseeds are highly empathic, especially to emotional energy. Prior to becoming aware of their abilities, many had problems differentiating between other people's problems and their own. Unconsciously they have absorbed feelings of distress, anger, and other emotions from others. This usually amplifies their own feelings and causes confusion. For this reason, Pleiadian starseeds have a strong tendency to suffer from depression and emotional and mental blocks or issues. On top of all that, the majority of starseeds have sensitive bodies, and if they take prescribed medication to treat their so-called mental issues, they may have terrible side effects.

Sadly, most Pleiadian starseeds endure abusive childhoods where they are mistreated emotionally, physically, and/or sexually. This pattern of abuse typically continues throughout their teenage years and adulthood. They may rebel in their teens, attempting to "find" themselves. Eventually this will trigger an awakening in them; these unpleasant events have taken place and they are ready to take their power back and end any mistreatment.

When a pleasant childhood is experienced, a significant event might arise later in life. Unfortunately, this event may rattle their emotions and nervous system to the point that they suffer a breakdown. When this happens they are pushed to reach out for help and they begin to search for their true life purpose. Once they find out who they really are, they are ready for a new beginning. Their life on Earth will be blissfully beautiful when it's fully understood.

In their personal lives, Pleiadian starseeds are wonderful and loyal life partners but usually attract people with emotional problems. Before they understand their ability to feel the soul and the love energy, they might mistake these feelings for falling in love. Because of their loyalty, they might remain in unhappy relationships for many years or have difficulty understanding why their partner may have left them after they helped him or her.

From my experiences working with Pleiadian starseeds, those who have a single DNA are generally not inclined to have tattoos on their bodies. This is very interesting, and I personally do not have an interest at this time in body art. Those with merged DNA may like body art. (There will be a further discussion of tattoos in a later chapter.)

Another interesting similarity amongst Pleiadian starseeds is a love of dogs and a preference for gold over silver metal.

Pleiadian starseeds are natural soul healers. They make terrific energy healers, psychics, consultants, and life coaches. They can also be great artists or crystal jewelry makers, as they have the ability to combine the beauty of art with natural healing. Many of them work in the medical field and are in service to others. Should they not work directly in the healthcare industry, they gravitate toward holistic medicine and naturopathic healing. Many occupations will make them happy when they learn how to use their unique soul healing energy.

The sayings *Put your heart in all you do,* and *Put your soul in everything you do* are perfect descriptions of Pleiadian tendencies. As earlier mentioned, the main ability and mission of Pleiadian starseeds is connecting with the soul, bringing healing to the soul, and helping the soul spiritually grow. When healing is brought to the soul on a soul level, the healing descends into the physical body and the results are miraculous. Many diseases originate from the emotional and mental planes, and are then stored within one's soul energy. In order to heal the soul, one needs to learn to connect with it on a deep level. To Pleiadian starseeds this is a natural way of being.

PRACTICES FOR PLEIADIAN STARSEEDS

+ **Learning energy healing,** for example Reiki, Healing Touch, or Soul Healing, at least the basics of self-help, is a rescue remedy for Pleiadian starseeds. Energy healing helps you clear and balance and connects you more deeply with your higher self. The more you practice, the more benefits you'll receive. Working with the body's subtle energy systems you can remove blocks and stagnation, become aware of limiting patterns that need to be transformed, and replenish your energy.

+ **Performing work from the heart center** with compassion and understanding instead of the brilliant, logical mind of Pleiadians allows starseeds to share their soul healing energy in any profession. Feel love within your heart and let love be your guide in all that you do.

+ **Soothing the nervous system** with focused breathing and meditation, as used for example in yoga or qigong practice, may prevent Pleiadian starseeds from burn-out or a nervous breakdown, while teaching them to manage their own energy. Using the breath to relax and heal the body and mind is a very powerful practice. Feeling anxious or experiencing chronic stress can be quite destructive to the nervous system and to one's overall health. Taking the time to calm the nervous system helps us regain balance. Since daily stressors are a part of life, it is ideal to have a short, simple exercise that can be done anywhere to alleviate this stress.

✦ **Breathing deeply and consciously,** with steady, slow inhalations and exhalations, signals our nervous system that it is safe to shift from stress to tranquility. To begin: Breathe through your nose, inhaling for a count of three. Pause for a count of one, then exhale for a count of five. Pause for a count of one after the exhale. During this practice, let thoughts of peace fill your mind and body. Repeat the cycle, breathing this way for several minutes. You can adjust the count to make your breathing more comfortable while remembering to keep the exhale longer than the inhale. You'll notice an improvement in mood and serenity with this simple technique. When doing it at home, try this variation: Lie down, close your eyes, and add your favorite meditation, music, or nature sounds to the mix.

✦ **Connecting with a tree and drawing on its natural energy** can be extremely grounding. This can be done by practicing the Guardian Tree Exercise below. Have you ever talked to a tree? When growing up I had a special friend: a cherry tree that grew in my grandparents' backyard, which was filled with fruit trees. There were many lovely trees in the yard, but this one was special.

It was tall and you could climb up to the very top where the branches opened like a seat. I could sit there for hours and hide behind its leaves. In addition, it bore the sweetest, juiciest cherries when in season.

When I would climb my tree, the minute my hands touched its smooth bark I would feel a sense of belonging and understanding. It also filled me with wondrous waves of courage. The gentle spirit of the cherry tree filled me with hope; the future seemed brighter and dreams felt attainable. (I needed that.) There I would sit—feeling free, happy, and protected from the outside world. It was *my* safe place.

Once, when stretching up for a bunch of the ripest cherries, I slipped and began to fall from the tree, which was twenty feet tall. There were no branches below that would slow my free fall. After expecting the worst, somehow I landed on branches that had mysteriously appeared, like the arms of a caring parent. Those were the gentle arms of my tree. Shaken but unhurt, I was hardly scratched! Later, when climbing my tree again, I climbed up to the branch I had fallen off of. Looking down, all I could see was a wide-open space and a few thin branches swaying in the wind.

My belief has always been that the tree spirit of that tree protected me.

+ **Learning to open and close your energy** (page 35 in Andromeda)
+ **Visiting the beach, nature, and walking barefoot** (page 33 in Andromeda)

EXERCISE
✳ Finding Your Own Guardian Tree ✳

To have a guardian tree is a blessing! Your tree could become your very own important source of energy, to be used for meditation, healing, energizing, strengthening, and protection. Once you find your tree you can always connect with it, even at a distance, simply by imagining a picture of it in your mind. Trees are the highest species of plant growth evolution, as they usually live much longer than plants and flowers. Many legends exist about their wisdom. In ancient times trees were thought to have souls. Their energy naturally varies from tree to tree, thus you need to find a tree that makes you feel good and that you are most drawn to.

Take a walk in nature and find a tree that you are instantly drawn to. The type of tree or what it looks like is not important. Pick one that makes you feel good when you are next to it.

After you choose your perfect guardian tree, place your hands on its trunk and hug your tree like you would your best friend. You can also stand or sit with your spine up against it.

Closing your eyes, focus on the tree and its energy. Ask your tree if you can connect with his or her energy. You will feel a very wonderful energy flowing through you; that is your yes sign.

Now take a few full deep breaths, breathe your tree in, relax, and let go of the mind's chatter. Find the harmony between you and your tree. Imagine being one with the tree, feeling its energy, becoming one with the tree energy and taking in as much of its energy as you wish. You do not need to be worried about taking too much.

As the tree offers its energy to you, be open to receiving thoughts, feelings, or images in your mind. You can talk with your tree as you would to a friend by talking about your worries, hopes, and wishes. Trees are very happy to communicate with us.

Communicate with him or her (your tree may have male or female energy or both) either in your mind or aloud; whatever feels comfortable. Notice how this tree makes you feel: Does it have a name? Does it have a message for you?

Tell your tree that you like its energy; you can express love for the tree and ask the spirit of the tree, if possible, to connect with it at other times and draw on its energy. If you want to invite this energy into your house, ask the spirit of the tree to envelop your home.

When you are ready, make a memory that will help you to "mentally" return to your tree. For example, remember your tree in your mind, note how it feels, smells, and how it makes you feel, or take a photograph of it.

Next time, when you're in need of increased energy, healing, or protection and you're not able to physically come to the tree, just recall it by focusing your mind on it by looking at the photo. Or focus your mental memory on the tree.

You can have as many trees as you like! When feeling ready, express your gratitude and give thanks to your tree. You may wish to leave a gift or a token. In native tradition for instance, one always gives something in return.

3
Sirius

S hining brighter than any other star in the sky is Sirius, a close neighbor to Earth. Sirius is visible in the northern hemisphere at night in winter. Just like Andromeda and the Pleiades, it became home for many Lyrans after the destruction of Lyra. Sirians and Lyrans developed an incredibly strong bond between them, becoming two peas in a pod.

THE SIRIAN BEINGS

The Sirius star nation beings are seekers of truth and knowledge. They are scribes of ancient records that are stored in the Library of Light and called the Akashic Records. This is where all of the Universal Light history records are collected.

Sirians are intellectual beings possessing a great demeanor and amazing self-control. They are often acknowledged as elders and respected for their ancient knowledge and wisdom. Most people think they are quiet, intellectual beings who spend much of their time in libraries. However, there is much more to Sirians than just well-kept books.

They are wonderful organizers known for their many uplifting spiritual ceremonies. Located on Sirius B is the Sacred Ceremonial Temple of the Sirius tribe, where many meetings with their starseed brothers and sisters, especially Pleiadians and Andromedans, take place. Together during their nighttime rituals they enjoy music, singing, dancing, and chanting. In these rituals, they wear clothes with little objects that make a soft clinking noise like bells. The sound of the bells carries through their world at celebratory times. They like to celebrate freedom in everything; even their clothing is light, comfortable, and loose around their bodies.

Sirians have incarnated on Earth from the time of its beginning. Many ascended masters and great minds come from a Sirian ancestral line. Most of the advanced technology found in ancient Egypt came from the Sirian and Orion beings that either visited or incarnated to assist a thriving new world. In the time after the cataclysm, their goal was to preserve knowledge from ancient Atlantis in several parts of the Earth, where it would be accessible for future generations to recover if we were to forget who we are, where we came from, and what our skills and abilities are.

Ancient knowledge is one of the profound abilities Sirians retain. Similarly to their Andromedan or Pleiadian star brothers and sisters, they are gifted energy healers. It is quite common for Sirians to be more involved in healing on an intellectual level than a hands-on level, however. Often they develop into teachers of the healing arts instead of healers themselves. Sirians are seekers of knowledge who effortlessly study at several universities in various star nations. They master their signature abilities mostly so as to understand them, so they can correctly document them in the Book of Light.

Ancient Sirians on Earth are known to be Lemurians and/or Atlanteans. According to legend, when the big flood came, Lemurians were led to live and thrive underground. After the flood, they emerged from the inner Earth and were known as natives whose mission was to bring wisdom, knowledge, healing, and technology to the planet. It has been said that some ancient Lemurians still live in the Crystal Cities in the inner Earth, together with other beings.

Sirian starseeds have a special connection to Lemurian crystals because they encoded them with light codes of ancient knowledge. The purpose of storing light codes within crystals was to literally create "time capsules" that can be accessed at any given time. Sirians know that during an incarnating process, all beings of a higher vibration have to lower their vibration into the 3D reality of the Earth realm to be able to sustain the physical body. Lowering a vibration can cause conflict in the conscious soul memory and result in "soul amnesia" (not being able to remember who you are). That is what we are still experiencing today. Thus, the Sirians grandfathered an idea of storing messages in the Earth realm. These messages were stored in many various crystals and stones in order to give us "messages from our soul family"—to help us remember who we are and what we need to know.

THE HOME WORLD

Sirius has several planets. All of them have vast forests, oceans, rivers, and lakes. Life varies somewhat from planet to planet. On journeys with my guides and clients, I have always been taken to Sirius B. With gratitude, I have learned that my abilities allow me to access all of its information. Sirius B is home to the Sirians' Sacred Ceremonial Temple, several Light Libraries, and an Akashic Records library.

During a soul journey with Tanya, a Sirian starseed, and our guides, we entered Sirius B, where Tanya's soul family welcomed us. They led us through gardens and toward a long path that appeared to be built from one smooth stone. The path was wide (about fifteen feet or so) and actually made up of stone steps that slid into one another. The color of the stones was light and comparable to Earth's granite. The path had nice smooth edges leading up to an enormous building with many circular towers that resembled balconies.

The guides telepathically communicated with us and shared how all the buildings in the Sirius system are made using sacred geometrical patterns. Sacred geometry is used for its energy properties. When used correctly, sacred geometry can align with other natural elements and work as an amplifier of energies. Sacred geometry has many properties and there are multiple uses for it.

LIBRARY OF LIGHT

Together we entered the great hall of the Library of Light, home of all records since the beginning of time. Typically it is viewed as a building or time machine, allowing travel to anywhere in the past. While entering we felt as though the whole universe had swallowed us up. Imagine being inside a spaceship traveling through the universe; being inside viewing the wonders of space through an enormous window!

Next, we headed toward a room containing light records, given that our guides wanted to share how to retrieve information with us. They pointed out that because of a Free Will Law, we were able access any information we desired. While there, our energy was greatly enhanced, allowing us to learn all that we desired.

If you undertake the same journey you will start to feel plugged into the universal energy flow, knowing and understanding anything you want. When you are done receiving the light record information, how much knowledge you retain (in your conscious mind) will depend on your own light energy and your mind's capacity for it. This truly depends on whether or not individuals can keep this information in their own "information system."

This means that when you meditate and access information with the assistance of your guides and then come back to your physical energy, you may not remember all the information that you felt you knew. All the information you gained in your meditating journey is stored in your unconscious memory, even though your conscious mind cannot instantly recall it.

Forgetfulness is common because knowledge should be protected. When you are evolved enough to use and share all the ancient information with integrity, honesty, and for the highest benefit to the universe, you will remember everything.

Another reason for forgetfulness is that you are accessing higher dimensional vibrations or knowledge and then lowering it down to the 3D physical reality. Once again, your own vibrations will need to be higher. For example, you may need to go through an ego-transforming journey before remembering ancient truths. It is necessary for you to work on your light body, preparing your physical vessel so that you may hold this higher vibrational information within, and then use it for the good of others.

Even though our journey in the Library of Light was relatively short, the amount of knowledge our guides shared with us was astounding. I just knew this was going to be a wonderful experience for us both! Tanya was able to reconnect with her star family and I was taught wonderful information to share with all of you!

TWIN FLAME TEMPLE

For the next leg of our journey we were teleported to a very sacred place called the Twin Flame Temple. We entered an ancient bathhouse with a huge pool in its center. The temple was circular in shape with a high ceiling resembling the flower of life but with eight leaves. The center outline of the flower of life symbol connected to the eight columns of the temple. The columns were not straight but gently arched and twisted. Below, in the center, was a bright, light blue pool. Although we were alone, Tanya felt invited to enter the pool and gently lowered herself into it. Intuitively I sensed the essence of lotus flowers. They were not visible, but I sensed the water was infused with their essence. Tanya was informed that this was a cleansing bath, offered to her because this was her first conscious journey to Sirius.

To our surprise, a man walked into the pool and introduced himself as her twin flame. I saw their soul energies join instantly. There was an overwhelming feeling of love and unity but not in a sexual way. It was a feeling of belonging and understanding; it was a sense of eternity. Their energy became one, not only as two beings, but also as one with everything. I sensed that the water element was very important to this energy of oneness. A high percentage of our physical body is composed of water and water is a natural amplifier, thus twin flame energy is projected into the physical body. (Note: Shortly after our session, Tanya fell in love.)

Our guides shared with us that connecting to twin flame energy has much more importance than we think. On Earth we confuse our sexual desire or feeling the need to be in love with a need to connect with our twin flame. Our guides shared with us that it should not matter if you physically connect with your twin flame or not in your Earth life. It should not matter if he or she has incarnated in the same time frame as you. Instead, it's important to consciously connect to each other's energy.

It is possible to consciously connect to your twin flame through the everlasting energy of your own soul. You can support each other's energies, endeavors, and life mission. Remember that you are one, part of each other, and both of you have embarked on a learning journey. This learning journey may also include connecting with your soul mates, sharing energy, and being happy without physically reconnecting with your twin flame at this time. Just your acceptance that you could connect with your twin flame and have always been connected to him or her can make an important difference to your own energy.

This is comparable to the energy leap of finding and reconnecting with your soul family (or your awakening)! Your heart should not bleed with pain and yearning for your twin flame because that will cause emotional distraction and you might be missing the great mission of your life. Your souls are always connected, and you are always together! You may live in different lifetimes, have different families and friends, yet the essence of your twin souls will always be together until you both are ready to be one.

The more you realize this, the more love and joy you will bring into your life. You will realize that there is no need to feel jealous, possessive of one another, or controlling. There is no need to feel alone if you have not found your twin flame in this realm yet. You need to learn to love yourself, love your soul, and love everything about you! When you learn to love from the level of your soul you will empower yourself, you will master unselfish self-love, and you will inspire others to do the same. Allow yourself to love fully, including everyone and everything around you, without judgment. When you are full of love, your heart will overflow with abundance and joy.

Please know that your twin flame is experiencing the same. He or she is a part of you, as you are part of him or her. When the right time comes, you will reunite again fully.

SACRED GEOMETRY IN ARCHITECTURE

Upon leaving the Twin Flame Temple we viewed several building structures that resembled ancient Chinese homes with layered roofs bending slightly upward as well as the ancient Italian building known as the Leaning Tower of Pisa. Our guides explained that Sirians helped to combine architectural styles from all across the universe to influence Earth's own evolution and growth. When starseeds from various star nations incarnate on Earth, they have many reminders of who they are and where they came from standing right in front of their eyes. The guides showed us a few building structures until we understood the idea that "energy structures" were built all over the world. To some they are just buildings, but to those who are sensitive to energy they are infused with the ancient energy and knowledge that unconsciously speaks to them. When you are ready you will consciously access and understand this energy and meaning. This is true for crop circles also. To some they are skillful art and to others they hide coded messages. The question is, are you evolved enough to read and understand the message?

ALTEN TEMPLE

Visiting Alten Temple was a very different experience. From the outside, the temple looked like a giant cone pointing to the sky. The temple was a dark maroon color and had a "ring" around it close to its bottom, just above its entrance. I noticed some symbols and letters of the Language of Light on its sides.

Andromeda's whale and dolphin beings, guardians of the Alten Temple, welcomed us inside. The temple serves as a healing and meeting place for the Council of Light as well as for council meetings and lectures. The bottom of the temple connects to the sea, where these beings can happily live in their natural habitat. Many beings from other star nations travel here to work in scientific laboratories.

On our journey we were led to the healing chamber. When we entered it our attention was directed to an octagon-shaped wheel that was in the center of the room. This wheel had eight very comfortable seats inside. When taking a seat we "sank" into the cushions that wrapped around us as we were buckled in. We felt safe even though the straps were not visible; we intuitively knew this wheel would spin very fast, like an amusement park ride. We were very comfortable knowing the other side of this octagon connected to water and was operated by dolphin and whale beings.

After safely securing us, the guides left the room and the octagon wheel gently moved. In the center was another device that moved forward and had light extending from it. This was a healing light, which we learned was used for deep healing purposes, especially for healing the physical body. When leaving, we felt absolutely refreshed and rejuvenated.

SIRIUS'S HELP TO EARTH

Sirians inhabit the star nation that understood how to infuse Earth with their ancient energy so that other generations could easily access it and remember or recall the "old energy." Just as Lyrans were inventors of DNA merging, Sirians are the masterminds behind preserving memory and energy within the depths of the Earth. They preserved their ancient energy in buildings such as the pyramids. They also concealed much information within the Earth's body, soil, water, and stone.

The Sirians' message is, "Be one with nature. Understand that nature and you are one with the universe, and one with us."

The soul journey with Tanya was enlightening to both of us. Through her journey, I could affirm the information that Sirians had shared with me in the past.

ENERGY POWER CENTER (EPC)

A Sirian's EPC is located in its sixth chakra, with its strongest psychic energy centered in the third eye. A Sirian's sense of hearing and smell is tremendous. Usually Sirian starseeds can easily view such things as auras, energy, and spirits. They can communicate telepathically, remote view, and tele-transport to different places. Their psychic and cognitive abilities are astonishing. If their DNA merges with that of other star nations or they study at other star nation universities, they acquire that star nation's abilities as well.

SIRIAN STARSEEDS ON EARTH

Sirian starseeds have beautiful, strong, and grounded warrior energy. They have a huge urge to help people and fight for their rights. Others perceive them as very strong, not by size but mentally. They look and act as if they are not afraid of anything, yet their soul is undoubtedly gentle, full of light and kindness, and they too have worries. They are sensitive empaths, similar in this way to their starseed brothers and sisters, and they need kindness and love to thrive. One of their great passions is reading books on their many interests.

One common thing I have noticed about these starseeds is that they are somehow more resilient to negative energies. This is because their EPC is located in their sixth chakra. Therefore, even though they have great empathic ability, they do not sponge all the negative energy into the heart chakra as the Pleiadians do. Nor do they absorb these energies into their solar plexus like Andromedans do. They do not feel as confused about negative energies as the Pleiadians and Andromedans did before their awakening. Many times they go through states of confusion about who they are and what their mission is. They may try to join several different religious groups and explore various spiritual beliefs and teachings in a quest to find themselves.

Sirian starseeds use a great amount of logic to solve everything. This is good and bad, depending on the state of their awakening.

The bad part is that it takes them longer to realize that they are different from others (that they are starseeds) and to know that not everything can be explained by logic. The good part is that once they awaken, they can logically combine amazing ancient energies with the present time and apply the results to our world in a way we can understand. Some Sirian starseeds such as Nikola Tesla, Albert Einstein, and many others might have felt they were born ahead of their time. However, the work they shared with us has been perfectly timed. We are ready to continue with this amazing work, just as we do now for example, with Essene energies that are more than two thousand years old.

Sirian starseeds are attracted to native teachings. They often choose to study indigenous forms of energy work, shamanism, and herbal healing. Many Sirian starseeds also resonate with Pagans. They are very sensitive and have a special connection to all elements of the Earth, nature, crystals, and animals. From my readings, I've also found that the majority of Sirian starseeds are cat lovers! Cats remind them of their Lyran friends. Some Lyran beings also incarnate as cats of all sizes on Earth to assist their Sirian starseed friends to adjust in their human body vessel. Sirian starseeds are naturally interested in Egypt and the pyramids, with many of them experiencing a past lifetime in Egypt.

Since Sirians love reading and sharing knowledge, many of them become writers, leaders, inspirational talkers, newswriters, and broad-casters, as well as inventors, scientists, and physicists. Their warrior spirit might also attract them to the military, security forces, the police force, and legal work. Some Sirian starseeds devote their life to teaching children and youth. They enjoy an educational role and can easily create a special connection with kids. More and more children are born almost awakened and need someone who can understand them on a starseed level. A highly intelligent starseed child may be labeled a troublemaker or a kid with ADD or ADHD. These kids are likely to speak their mind, are different on many levels, and are sensitive to various emotions and their environment. They need to be understood as well as put on the right life path.

Their personality is composed of both fun and seriousness. One part is focused on study and work, as they strongly feel that they have to achieve something and often have good motivation to do so. The other part of their personality loves fun, music, and dancing, the company of good friends, and/or being silly, perhaps even a tiny bit eccentric.

Interestingly, many Sirians I have worked with love cheese, natural food (especially fruit), water, and rainbows, as these things remind them of home. They have an equal preference for gold and silver metal. Several starseeds I've known have entered the military although few remain in it, often leaving the service feeling broken inside. Somehow military life is not what they'd expected it to be. They love freedom and are willing to fight to the death for the right reason. They have a tendency to be pulled into conspiracy theories and a few brave ones have uncovered the truth and shared it with others despite the consequences. Their warrior spirit does not care what might happen to them. They feel strongly that they must share the truth they know or uncover.

Sirian starseeds have brilliant minds. They need to learn to bring the energy from the mind into the entire physical body and practice "whole body intuition." That means learning to sense energy throughout their whole body, not just with their mind. Their mission on Earth is to make our lives easier with their inventions, new technology, science, truth, teachings, and healing. Sirians know how to use ancient knowledge and make it futuristic.

PRACTICES FOR SIRIAN STARSEEDS

+ **Learning about ancient structures and places** on Earth is key, for these sacred sites hold transformational powers. They have the capacity to awaken and transform consciousness and increase wisdom, peace, and intuition. Sirian starseeds have the capability to see with their inner mind hidden messages in these sites and to decode them and share them with humanity.

The strong energetic field of these sites is amplified by the countless sages, healers, and seekers who have journeyed there. Meditating and praying, they have continuously added to each site's remarkable power. Locations favored by Sirians include pyramids, megalithic stone circles, ceremonial sites, sacred mountains, bodies of water, forest groves, temples, shrines, and places aligned with star systems, planets, and celestial regions.

Choosing one or several sites that resonate with you is a very powerful thing to do as well. Read about them, gather pictures of them, watch videos about them, and then in a relaxed meditative state, create a clearly focused intention to travel there in spirit. See and feel yourself immersed in the sights, sounds, and energy of the place. For guidance on a particular topic, ask for insight and remain open to the messages from the wisdom teachers and ascended masters whose unique energetic frequencies are present there.

+ **Researching warriors,** their characteristics, how you can learn from them, and meeting challenges the way a warrior would is also beneficial. This is because as a Sirian starseed these traits are encoded in your DNA. Warriors have the qualities of courage, discipline, perseverance, and impeccable ethics. They are self-assured, possess an expanded awareness, and handle adversity well. Warriors never overreact; instead, they strategically know when to take action, and when to wait and let a situation unfold. Having the gifts and traits of a warrior can help us in many circumstances. Begin by making statements of intention and picturing yourself successfully embodying the qualities you desire. Imagining in advance how you will respond to a situation brings added clarity and self-confidence.

+ **Reviewing your life** and the things you've learned and setting new intentions is germane. Combine all that you've learned and let go of what no longer serves you in a positive way. When you let go, you open yourself to be a true seeker of ancient knowledge who can rekindle wisdom teaching, healing modalities, medicine, science, technology, and more.

Suggested steps for your review:

+ Conduct an honest review of your life choices (both good and bad).
+ Deeply accept yourself and surround yourself with unconditional love.
+ Extend forgiveness to yourself and others.
+ Surrender, turning everything over to divine wisdom and guidance.
+ Recognize what may be new possibilities and opportunities in your life.
+ Plan your new intentions and visualize them, adding positive emotions when you're envisioning.
+ Make conscious, positive choices with the honesty and integrity to manifest each new intention.
+ Hold the frequency of the new affirmation or choice and think of it as being already accomplished.
+ Feel a sense of gratitude, which energizes the manifesting process.

+ **Visiting the beach, nature, and walking barefoot** (page 33 in Andromeda)
+ **Soothing the nervous system** (page 45 in The Pleiades)
+ **Connecting with crystals** (page 74 in Centaurus)

EXERCISE
✳ Sacred Space to Heal Sadness ✳

Find a quiet place. Take a deep breath in and release all the air out. Relax. Call for a Sirian guide from the highest available vibrations to assist you on this journey. Imagine that you are walking with your guide on a path toward a waterfall.

You can see gray boulders resting one on top of the other. The crystal-clear water is falling down over them into a little pool of water. You can sense the water; you can literally feel how clear and pure it is. You can remember that water used to be so pure on Earth a long time ago. You know that you are in a sacred place.

You sit down beside your guide to enjoy the serenity and peace. Everything is quiet. The only sound you hear is water falling on the stones. The sound resonates with your soul.

Here you have an opportunity to reflect on your sadness and to allow your mind to quiet down. Take as long as you need. Look back at your life and see/feel/sense what makes you sad. Give yourself time to understand the root of your sadness. Allow yourself to accept all that has happened. When you are ready to accept your life, you are ready to move into forgiveness. Forgive yourself and others for everything that happened.

When you feel ready, take a small stone that is there by your side, then, having reflected and understood your life, give your sadness to this stone. This sad emotional energy will be transformed into the stone. You are ready for the transformation. You are ready to leave the sadness behind and the stone is ready to accept it. You do not need it anymore.

When you are ready, allow your Sirian guide to walk you back into the present time. Thank your guide and everyone who has assisted you. Stretch your legs and arms and take a deep breath in and enjoy your happy life!

PART TWO

Understanding

4

Centaurus

Centaurus is a bright constellation that can be found in the southern sky. Some well-known stars that appear in this constellation are Beta Centauri (also called Hadar), Proxima Centauri, and Alpha Centauri (also known as Rigel Kentaurus). Alpha Centauri happens to shine the brightest in this particular star pattern.

Eons ago, the Centaurian constellation was a pristine world inhabited by peaceful reptilian and dinosaurian beings. At the end of the Lyran wars, the Lyrans' peaceful arrival to Centaurus marked profound changes, both spiritual and technological. Soon thereafter, Andromedan, Sirian, and Pleiadian beings joined the Lyrans in Centaurus. Centaurus is recognized as the origin of the first hybrid beings.

THE CENTAURIAN BEINGS

Centaurian beings are wise teachers who often enjoy sharing their wisdom with others. They love to learn and teach. Ancestry, history, as well as all forms of art and music are core foundations of their curriculums. Fear, control, and physical arguments are not tolerated. They became masters in applying intellect and grace in order to win any argument. The presence of their energy vibrates unconditional love that allows you to merge into a deep spiritual journey of acceptance and forgiveness that will help you to transform your life and find your true self. Some Centaurians incarnate as animals on Earth and in other places in the universe.

The Lyra star nation is one of the oldest star nations in the galaxy. The Lyran race closely resembles the human race; they are fairly similar in appearance. Their home world was destroyed during the galactic star wars and they desperately needed a new home. The Lyrans negotiated with the Council of Light to settle on various planets and to begin a new journey on the path of light. They did not want to be part of any wars and their new mission was universal peace. Shortly after meeting with the Centaurian Council, which is located on Alpha Centauri, they received an invitation to populate this pristine constellation. Thus two very different kinds of star nations began a new journey: highly evolved human hybrids and intelligent and peaceful reptilians and dinosaurians (please note there are many different kinds of reptilian energies). Lyrans found a way to harmonize their cultures and teachings. They cocreated an astonishingly unique world.

As time went on, Lyrans campaigned for the idea of allowing various star nations to merge (combine) their DNA. (DNA carries the unique abilities of each star nation.) The campaign was received positively across the universe and Centaurus became one of the first home worlds to create star beings with merged DNA. The Council of Light also invited Andromedan, Sirian, and Pleiadian star nations to join in the project that had started making profound changes throughout the universe. Later on more star nations began to participate. Many new universities were created in the Centaurus constellation with each teaching being tailored for specific purposes. The beautiful beings with merged DNA eventually moved to various constellations in the universe, including Earth. These hybrids began incarnating on Earth in the mid-Atlantean era to assist in the growth and evolution of the human race.

There are various possibilities of DNA combinations of starseeds from Centaurus. Original Centaurians have reptilian or dinosaur DNA. After the introduction of DNA merging, new types of star beings were born. They include Lyran/Centaurian reptilian, Pleiadian/Centaurian reptilian, Lyran/Sirian/Centaurian reptilian, and Andromedan/Centaurian dino.

Summed up, the purpose of the DNA merge was to eventually end the galactic wars. The original plan was to create spiritual superwarriors who, gifted with various abilities, would lead the nations through spiritual transformation and into everlasting peace. (More information about DNA merging and its purpose can be located in chapter 6.)

The Lyran/Sirian/Centaurian reptilian or Andromedan/Centaurian dino types are mostly focused on science, technology, research, and leadership, while the Lyran/Andromedan/Pleiadian/dino, Andromedan/dino, or Pleiadian/dino are more interested in holistic healing, maintaining healthy environments, and preserving organic life. The Centaurian/ dino DNA is deeply connected to our animal kingdom, while the Centaurian/reptilian DNA offers a protective coating, to some degree, against negative energy.

Centaurians never embraced certain blueprints for living in a diverse society as other star nations did (for example: Lyran/Sirian and Andromedan/Pleiadian). Instead they created a unique Centaurian structure, which could be referred to as a flexible structure. This flexible structure is a combination of philosophy, history, and the teachings of Centaurian natives and all of the star nations living in their constellation. Each individual is celebrated and encouraged to evolve by way of their own inner guidance. This is quite different from other star nations who like to have a set structure to follow.

These star beings are acclaimed researchers who put a huge emphasis on art and music. Music and sound to them is like air to us. It is essential for living.

Centaurian hybrids love—and I emphasize the word *love*—to study. Almost always they choose to study about other star nations in-depth and learn their signature abilities, for example healing, science, and telepathy (to name a few). They master these abilities to the extent that if someone meets them, they could easily pass for a member of that particular star nation.

Centaurians have shared with me that even though they undergo huge changes while merging their DNA, they prefer to reproduce naturally. Old-fashioned bonding in families is important. They may have multiple partners in their family (males and females); however, there is no dominance in gender or any jealousy—with the result being that families live out their lives in beautiful harmony.

THE HOME WORLD

When I am working with Centaurian starseeds, I mainly connect to Alpha Centauri. I perceive Alpha Centauri to be a capital city (planet) for Centaurian beings as it is home to the Centaurian council. Alpha Centauri also serves as a memory bank for this constellation. Here information on all Centaurian history is stored, which is a little unusual. Instead of creating records, documents, art, or any form of record keeping, the energy records of Alpha Centauri work as part of the Universal Mind, which can be accessed through higher vibrational intelligence. Centaurus is a heaven for hybrids who are thirsty for diverse knowledge. Thus, there you will find thousands of universities from various star nations, each featuring the particular home-world energies and signature teachings.

Learning the past and ancient history has significant value to all Centaurian beings. They have dedicated DNA teachers who are experts in ancestry and history. They have learned that creating hybrid beings is a physical process. However, the soul of this being is so diverse and sensitive that it needs to be carefully nourished so that it can stay peaceful and loving instead of feeling confused.

On planet Hadar you will meet amazing psychologists who teach about the past. They promote forgiveness and acceptance and seek understanding as to how and why we should all accept each other and our ancestral mistakes. They lovingly embrace everyone's mistakes and debate about them at length until the root of the problem is found and sorted out so that repetition of the mistake will be prevented. The philosophy behind this is that we can all learn from past mistakes and cocreate a future we truly desire.

The Centaurus constellation has many places to visit, the appearances of which vary dramatically with each planet. You can see huge water worlds with rivers, magnificent waterfalls, desert-like lands, jungle forests, muddy swamps, and fertile land where the most amazing plants and herbs grow. The Centaurus constellation also features fancy cities.

Centaurians love art and music. I believe that Hathors have a connection to this place. Sound frequencies are carried in the air, like oxygen is on Earth. This is relaxing, healing, nurturing, and joyful. Each individual can tune the sound or frequency to their own needs or liking.

You may choose to listen to the music telepathically, out loud, or experience sound vibrations throughout your body. When you listen to the sounds, they feel like one long tone or melody that is merging into another. It is difficult to describe, for we don't have complete knowledge of this kind of sound here on Earth. This kind of sound gently teaches the body to become more sensitive (opening all sensory systems) and directs the soul to higher vibrations. In this the sound functions like a fine-tuning fork with the ability to heal body, mind, and spirit.

The Centaurian constellation is full of wonder and unexpected excitement and is the most diverse, peaceful place in the universe.

ENERGY POWER CENTER (EPC)

As with a correct identification of DNA, naming the right Energy Power Center for Centaurian starseeds may be challenging.

The main EPC for all Centaurians is the fifth chakra; there are additional EPCs that may be easily merged with the main EPC.

Those with reptilian DNA have an EPC in their sixth chakra. Those with dino DNA have merged third and fourth chakras. There is an additional chakra between the stomach and heart center; its color is turquoise. This particular chakra is found in animals on Earth and can serve to activate and communicate light between humans and animals. In 2013, this energy was consciously activated for our use. It also activated animals and was used to communicate telepathically. Before that it had just been asleep, waiting to be put to use.

Hybrids may have several EPCs. For example, Sirian/reptilian hybrids will have a fifth- and sixth-chakra EPC; Lyran/dino will have a whole-body EPC with a special focus on third-, fourth-, and fifth-chakra EPC, and Andromedan/dino a third-, fourth-, and fifth-chakra EPC. There are many possibilities. These EPCs can work independently of each other or be merged into one.

I have noticed that one EPC usually is stronger than the others. This has a lot to do with each individual's past lives, childhood traumas, and current life. When healing is achieved in these individuals, they are ready to have another EPC activated. Eventually, all EPCs are activated and used as needed.

CENTAURIAN STARSEEDS ON EARTH

Centaurian starseeds have been incarnating on Earth since the time of Atlantis; however, many hybrids began to arrive *after* its destruction. I always sense their incarnation in Egypt. They came here to share with us sacred knowledge, to improve our science and technology, and to teach energy-healing modalities. One important part of their mission is to transmute negative energy into light from all elements and beings, in peaceful, noninvasive ways.

In my psychic readings I have noticed a pattern with my Centaurian starseed clients that led me to the conclusion that they are amazing researchers. This ability allows them to find desired information in a very short time.

In the beginning of their individual awakening these starseeds have no particular focus; they just sponge in information. Often they have an unexplained urge to learn various healing forms, study metaphysics, and explore their spirituality by studying various religions. They learn whatever they can put their hands or mind to and feel they need to search for more. They are not easily content and commonly feel like something is missing. Intuitively they know there is only a little bit of truth in each of the world's religions or belief systems. This is frustrating and some of them feel lost for a long time as a result.

Centaurian starseeds (often those with Andromedan or Pleiadian hybrid DNA) become very passionate about the art of healing, which they tend to have a natural gift for. These healers usually had a very traumatic childhood on Earth and experienced difficulty growing up. Remembering their passion for the healing arts helps them to heal their soul and physical body, if needed.

Some starseeds, especially those with reptilian-merged DNA, have had violent past lives on Earth (not within the universe) and now need to remember them. Often this is hard and difficult to accept: that a being of light, which they truly are, might have done something negative in the past. This feeling and knowledge may lead to depression. They may be afraid of themselves and question their character and whether or not they are worthy enough to help others. Yet they have a burning desire to assist others on their journey. Often this causes an internal pull about which way to go. Sometimes they might fall into addiction in order to still any memories that stem from the subconscious mind, which they can't consciously understand.

There is a very good reason why they have had a violent past. It's not because they are bad, rather it's to acquire experience. They have chosen the experience by employing their free will. Some of these beings of light have agreed to take on a very bad incarnation and to hurt others to experience the dark side. Centaurians came to Earth to assist in the transformation of dark energy to light energy, especially in this particular lifetime. They volunteered to assist formerly dark beings to fully adjust to the light energy. I emphasize that they *needed* to go through a dark experience to fully understand and know how the dark side operates and how it controls and instills fear in the mind. After this knowledge is gained, these individuals can assist in freeing souls and assisting them on a journey of transformation.

To put it into simple words, for example, sometimes the best drug-abuse counselors are the ones who have had addictions themselves. These starseeds have the ability to drain others of negative energy and transform it into positive energy. This is a very difficult task and can't be performed by just any being.

There are various races of reptilians and their personalities vary. Centaurian reptilians are beings of light. It is important to note that they are transformers of negative energy, instead of the fighters of it as are some other reptilian races who serve the light side.

Earlier in the book we discussed body art, and I wanted to add to that discussion here. I've noticed that those who have stronger reptilian DNA may have an obsession with tattoos and a deep need to express themselves with writing or pictures on her or his body. This desire usually has a deeper meaning for these starseeds, such as a wish to express some inner turmoil or newly obtained wisdom. Or the impulse could stem from a past life as something remembered but not completely understood. Unconsciously or consciously, this application of tattoos may help them to recall who they are and what their purpose is. Some do not like to expose tattoos on their skin, but still find the idea interesting and like it on others.

Those who have stronger dino DNA tend to have a deep connection with animals and nature. Often their traumatic past history on Earth leads them to the animal world where they can discover their own abilities and also where they can heal. It's common for some of these beings to have incarnated as animals in the past. Other star nations also incarnate on Earth in the form of animals, to assist starseeds on their life path. Animal incarnations have a lower vibration than that of the human form, and it is a challenging life for star beings. These incarnated animal beings need assistance as well and usually Centaurians are the ones to help. Because of their dino DNA and natural understanding of animals, they are amazing animal healers and communicators.

I also noticed a pattern that those with dino DNA tend to be "animal whisperers," that is, they can clearly hear what animals are expressing and are able to assist them on a deep level. We are moving into the time when we need to learn how to heal through the animals and vice versa—for animals to heal through us. The animal kingdom has endured much trauma on Earth and the Centaurians, alongside other star nations, are assisting in their healing.

Centaurian starseeds possess deep kindness, compassion, understanding, and love for others. They are intelligent, and their manner is often shy and humble, yet some Centaurian starseeds could be quite eccentric at times. When you talk with them, they have a royal presence about them. After awakening and comprehending their abilities, they are able to align their energy and combine all of the knowledge and experience they have gathered while learning many different things. These starseeds make wonderful healers, counselors, ambassadors, entertainers, scientists, researchers, psychologists, doctors, and veterinarians.

PRACTICES FOR CENTAURIAN STARSEEDS

+ **Researching areas such as psychology, healing, and other star nations** is very gratifying for Centaurians because they are skillful researchers and are naturally inquisitive. They have a great deal of wisdom to offer, and they're interested in adding to that knowledge in areas that intrigue them. Gain more information in fields such as psychology, healing, techniques for transmuting darkness into light, social causes, or different star nations. As teachers and givers, Centaurians are sure to implement and pass along what they've learned for the benefit of others.

+ **Connecting with animals and the animal kingdom** is another wonderful thing for a Centaurian to do. As wonderful companions, teachers, and healers, animals enrich our lives in many ways. Spend time with them by volunteering at an animal shelter or wildlife rescue center, visiting a zoo, or taking your own pet outside to play in the great outdoors. Animals give us unconditional love, joy, and emotional honesty. They are resilient, loyal, and quite interested in communicating with us. When you're with them, become very observant, remaining open to what they're trying to convey. Center your focus on your turquoise chakra (the space between the third and fourth chakra) and listen and observe from there. The more you intuitively listen, the more information you'll gain as your sensitivity becomes heightened. Take the opportunity to sharpen your telepathic skills by interacting with the animal kingdom. Information can be received as thoughts, feelings, visual images, or symbols. When you feel a calling to work with animals or to give healing to animals, you can make a conscious connection between your turquoise chakra and the animal's turquoise chakra and send the light from your animal EPC to their animal EPC. While you are doing this you will automatically light-activate the animal. Just as we are going through a human evolution, animals are going through their own evolution. Some animals are reincarnated beings of light or have had a human life in the past. Light activation can assist them in remembering who they are on a soul level. Often our pets come into our lives to be our guides and spiritual protectors; our helpers. However, it may not only be our pets that desire the activation. The entire animal kingdom may need it too. This is why animal EPC was awakened in us and especially in Centaurian beings. When you work with tame animals, you can simply rest your hands on the animal's EPC and imagine a beautiful turquoise color exchange between you. When working with wild animals, for your safety, only do so at a distance. Please also remember that time and distance do not really matter in energy work. Once you activate an animal, you can enjoy telepathic communication with them and work to heal each other. You may be surprised by the kind of information you may receive. You may also realize that some animals might have a bigger desire to assist you in healing than you yourself have! Do not overthink this and enjoy your special time and closeness to nature and its inhabitants.

+ **Meditating in an open space in nature** is grounding as well. Begin by focusing on the sights and especially the sounds around you, as sound is like air to Centaurian beings. Let the sounds of nature fill you with contentment. Next, bring your attention to the present moment and allow any distracting thoughts to drop away. When your awareness is fully present, breathe deeply, visualizing stress and tension leaving your body with each exhalation. Then imagine a cord of energy running from the soles of your feet to the center of the Earth. Pull earth energy into your body and aura with each inhalation, and let the calming, grounding resonance of the Earth merge with your energy field. As natural healers with compassion and love for others, it is important for Centaurians to nourish and give to themselves as well. During your meditation, envision divine rays of unconditional love and kindness filling your heart area, then each cell of your body, and then your aura. Spend a few moments sensing the energy deeply replenishing your body and spirit.

+ **Connecting with trees and other plants and creating your garden** is very good for Centaurians. Everything in nature has its own unique frequency, and our energy field benefits from interacting with the vibrational fields of the natural world. A great way to connect is by visiting a park or botanical garden or by taking a walk through your neighborhood and sensing the energy of the trees and plants around you. Consider creating a garden such as an herb garden or flower bed. Indoor house plants can bring you beneficial energy all year long.

+ **Connecting with crystals** is beneficial as well. Crystals carry a very strong connection to the planet's natural energy and are valued for their cleansing, energizing, and healing properties. Select crystals with the properties you're looking for—the stones that will best serve your needs (for example, in reducing stress or improving creativity). Holding a crystal or placing it on your body enables it to positively interact with both your physical body and your aura. When you receive a new crystal, sit quietly and close your eyes, hold the crystal in the palm of your hand, and intuitively sense what it communicates to you.

+ **Visiting the beach and nature and walking barefoot** (Page 33 in Andromeda)

EXERCISE

✳ Connect with Your Galactic Guide ✳

You can record this meditation or just read the step-by-step version (very slowly).

Adjust your body and make yourself comfortable. Imagine that you are sitting in a pure golden column of light. The golden light energy is warm, soothing, and comfortable. You feel relaxed and safe.

Take a deep breath in and exhale all the air out. Take another deep breath in and exhale. Now take one more deep breath in and exhale. Feel your body relaxing.

Relax your legs, relax your belly, relax your shoulders, relax your arms, relax your neck, and relax your head. Feel all of your muscles relaxing.

Now focus on your breath.

Take a deep long breath in and exhale all the tension from your body.

Take another long breath in and breathe out your worries and expectations.

Imagine your mind and your body becoming calm and relaxed. Empty your mind and enjoy this quiet place. Stay in this serene, peaceful, relaxed state for a while. If any thoughts come into your mind, just acknowledge them and let them go.

Now let your mind drift into a peaceful sanctuary where nothing can ever bother you. This is your own unique, happy, and safe place. You can imagine your sanctuary as heaven, a blossoming garden, a forest, a waterfall, a rainbow, or a place filled with beautiful colors—whatever feels right to you.

This is your sacred place.

Go to your sanctuary and find a comfortable place to sit down. This is your place. You can design it any way you like. When you have made yourself comfortable, send out a telepathic thought to your guide to tell him or her that you are ready to meet them. If you like you can say it out loud: "I ask to be connected with my guide from my home world and I thank you for connecting with me."

Now imagine that your guide is coming toward you. Your guide will now stop in front of you so that you can see or sense his or her energy. Notice the energy you are connecting with; this is the energy from your home. Experience how it feels. If you are comfortable with his or her energy, invite them to sit beside you. If not, then ask for another guide.

Now notice any sensations. What do you see, feel, sense, smell, or hear? You may have a vivid experience or you might just feel a subtle energy. You might see a color, smell a flower scent, or feel a touch, for instance.

Try not to think about or analyze this moment. Do not question the reality of your experience at this time. You will remember it all later and can analyze it then. This is the time to make a connection.

You can ask your guide for his/her name. Do not listen just with your ears, listen with your heart, listen with your Energy Power Center, and listen with your body.

Let all your senses pick up on the answer. Ask your guide to show you how he or she will be communicating with you in the future.

You can ask your guide which planet or star nation he or she is from.

Now ask your guide to strengthen the connection between you both. Ask him or her to work with you on a daily basis. Your guide will create an energy spark from your home world; a ball of light that will enter your soul to activate your light codes. You can feel this light building up and, when you are ready, accept it. This energy from your home world will strengthen your connection and will assist you in developing your unique abilities. Feel the energy spark go into your Energy Power Center, then breathe in this light and feel it expanding in your body.

Enjoy this moment. When you feel ready to go, thank your guide and say goodbye, then gently come back to your physical body. Gradually move your fingers, your legs, and your body, and become aware of the room you are in.

Here are a few suggested questions for your guides:

+ What is your name?
+ Where do you come from?
+ Have you ever experienced Earth life?
+ How may I better connect with you?
+ How can you help me develop my psychic abilities?
+ What is my mission here on Earth?

It's a good idea to write down your experience. Sometimes things that don't make sense at the time may make sense later on.

You may like to eat a light snack or drink something so that your system will kick back in. If there is anything you encounter on your journey that makes you feel uncomfortable, just send it away. Say, "Go back to your creator." That is all.

5

Epsilon Eridani

The constellation of Epsilon Eridani is located between the Orion star system and the Taurus star system. It is an enchanting world of Epsilonian beings who closely resemble our human image. Since 2012 their spaceships have stayed near Earth. They observe human evolution and gently assist us in awakening our natural abilities.

THE EPSILON ERIDANI BEINGS

The Epsilon Eridani beings are famous for the logic that comes from their heart rather than their mind. They are master decision-makers, skilled in making conscious and compassionate judgments in any situation. They are magnificent mediators who often travel from planet to planet, all over time and space, so that they may negotiate peace and solve misunderstandings or wrongdoings. In resolving situations they don't use threats or violence. Rather they use wisdom energy that stems from the heart and they talk about a problem until it's satisfactorily resolved.

They became so exceptional at this skill that in their home world they teach, to other star nations, the science and technology of mediating from the heart. This heart science (every decision originates from the heart) is used in all aspects of life—from technology to science to healing.

Epsilon Eridani beings prefer to have a physical body and like to be called "people." When they refer to the heart, they are actually referring to the soul. They shared with me that their soul sits in their heart chakra and is interconnected with their physical heart. Connecting with the soul through the heart bypasses the ego and allows one to be in a higher vibrational state. The outcome allows all information and further decisions to be pure and clear.

Epsilonians do not discriminate between other beings. They embrace diversity and assist others in accepting the truth. Something that may be a truth to one may be different to another, and defining the truth may not be a simple thing, but more complex in nature. Every truth or belief has several components, creating a solid base from which to influence the outcome of a particular truth or belief. For example, you can imagine truth as a molecule. An Epsilonian's ability allows them to take apart this truth molecule and explore each atom of it separately. It's an extraordinary skill.

Let's imagine atoms in this truth molecule. Each atom represents a dot. The Epsilonian will examine each dot separately and determine if some of them require healing, technological adjustments, or cleansing. Perhaps they've already been adjusted. Together all these atoms create a molecule of absolute truth.

For an Epsilonian, creating the absolute truth has nothing to do with brainwashing or getting their own way. They are more than willing to negotiate the best options and show you the possible outcomes in different ways. Their technology, time travel, and long study of all the ancient star nations (light or dark) allows them to understand the importance of other beings—their originality, concerns, fears, and needs, and how Epsilon Eridani or other star nations can assist them in the most loving and noninvasive way.

Epsilon Eridani is also home to other star nation beings, especially Sirians and Andromedans. When the whole movement in the universe began and other star nations started to settle on various planets, Epsilon Eridani welcomed the Sirians and then later on the Andromedans into their home. After they negotiated these living agreements, Sirians and Andromedans brought their culture, technology, and teachings to be shared and combined with Epsilonians' unique abilities. As they naturally evolved, their energy, philosophy, and beliefs merged and literally became one. There was no separation between them, and the Warriors of Light were born! When the Lyrans introduced the merging of DNA, they all gladly joined in the project.

Some people like to spread rumors and doubts about our future contact with any extraterrestrial beings and their intent with us. I have connected with Epsilon Eridani people while giving home-planet readings to my clients, and I am convinced that people from Epsilon Eridani have only peaceful intentions for humanity.

When the time comes for us to live with other star nations in unity on Earth (or another planet), Epsilonians will be the ones who will help us to mediate our terms so we will all be content with the outcome.

They would like us to know that they would never use power to control us or use any violence to make us agree to terms. They will only assist us in negotiating the terms that will be suitable for all sides, just like when Sirians and Andromedans settled in their home world.

As an aside, in one of the readings I gave, an interesting question arose. Since Epsilonians like to call themselves humans, do they have separate genders like we do? Do they menstruate as we do, or reproduce as we do, for that matter? This question came from a lady who we believe is an Epsilonian starseed and with spiritual awakening developed a traumatic feeling connected to blood, particularly menstrual blood. Of course, there may be several reasons for her reaction. The most logical would be that the feeling was a past-life memory. In any event, both she and I wanted to know more about Epsilonians and their reproductive process and whether or not there could be some connection between humans and Epsilonians in this regard.

To be honest, I had never thought about this before. A while ago, however, some Centaurians shared with me that they like to reproduce like us. They carry the baby in the mother's womb and give birth vaginally, which the majority of star nations view as a very old-fashioned and unnecessary practice. Centaurians have male and female genders, and I assume the females would have a menstrual period, and that their bodies work similarly to ours regarding reproduction.

When I turned to the Epsilonians with this question, I sensed that they do reproduce by choice; however, they do this a little differently than Centaurians. The Epsilonians too have male and female genders. They told me that some star nation beings such as Virgos or Lyrans have both genders in one body.

Epsilonians romance each other like we on Earth do. They also connect sexually and likewise experience sensations of pleasure. Feelings of sexual energy are not stimulated only by physical contact, but also by a soul and mind connection. I would say that, like Tantra would teach us, they weave together the physical and the spiritual energies to become one with everything through the union of both polarities.

In their relationships they do not experience feelings of jealousy or emotional drama as we sometimes do in our love relationships. The union is either in harmony or it's not. If they feel that the relationship is not in harmony, they separate on amicable terms and support each other on their respective journeys.

However, with Epsilonians there is a difference in reproduction. Females do not have the monthly menstrual periods we are familiar with, yet this creates no imbalance for them. Their sexual organs, when matured (which would be around our sixty to eighty years of age), are fully functioning, but their reproductive organs are in a sleep stage. The babies are created by choice, not by accident. You might call this per fected planned parenthood. When a couple desires to have a baby, they consult a specialist doctor who awakens their reproductive organs, both in the male and female bodies.

Similar to in-vitro fertilization, to create a baby the eggs and sperm are collected and their union occurs in a laboratory. The embryo is then examined for possible genetic defects that might affect the health of the baby. If anything is detected the embryo is genetically modified to ensure that the baby's body is healthy and that the soul entering the body will be housed in a good vessel. The baby does not grow in the mother's belly, but in a special incubator.

Parents meditate prior to the conception, until the birth, in order to connect with and stay connected to the soul of their soon-to-be baby, to prepare him or her for their journey in the physical body. Then, as on Earth, the parents take on the responsibility of teaching their child until they are grown, and to share their unique life with them, which is not so different from familial life here on Earth.

I sense that some discomfort is experienced after the female body produces the eggs. Her system cleans itself in what we can call a menstrual period, and then her reproductive organs once again are placed in sleep mode by her specialist. One benefit of having one's reproductive organs in sleep mode is longevity.

THE HOME WORLD

The Epsilon Eridani planets vibrate in a range of beautiful colors. These colors are a feast for the eyes and nurture the soul as well. When I sense Epsilonians I receive images of shades of pink ranging from soft to vibrant, as well as greens. The energy in their home planet feels peaceful and serene. Their air is a little bit heavy for us to breathe, but it feels very clean. They shared with me that in the past the air was polluted and not healthy.

This changed in the age of technological invention and growth, where they learned to cleanse the air naturally. This allowed them to effortlessly produce healthy air for their dry land, and supply enough clean air for their underwater world.

I was guided to Erza. Erza closely resembles our Earth, with only a few differences. A clear daytime sky is a yellow, harvest moon color. I did not perceive feeling or seeing a sun as we know it here on Earth. In spite of this, the grass was a luscious green and the day felt like a pleasant, late spring afternoon. In Erza one can easily relax on the grass while gazing at the sky, which brings a feeling of comfort and inner peace.

A vast body of water covers a large part of their homeland. This, however, does not raise any concerns for them. They have the technology to build cities in which to live under the water's surface and to occupy places that we can only dream of. Long ago they lived only on dry land.

When other nations started to settle in, they welcomed this change and embraced the opportunity to learn and expand their knowledge and their technology. This allowed them to create what may seem to us to be impossible. This includes building humongous cities underwater that are powered by a means that we can only compare to solar energy.

Many wonderful new things started to happen in Epsilon Eridani that improved the quality of their home worlds significantly.

THE FLOWER LIBRARY

There are various fascinating places in Epsilon Eridani. Some are highly technically developed or futuristic while some closely resemble our world. I was shown the Flower Library on Erza. I learned that access to the Flower Library is granted to you only after you finish advanced studies. It made me wonder why, since on Earth it is common to visit the library often to find supportive material for your studies.

I was told by my guides that while you study you do not have a need to go into the Flower Library. You are receiving all the information you need from the educational source of your choice. This is supposed to help keep you focused on the chosen topic, as the Flower Library might be a distraction with its boundless material. I would like to make a little notation here that no study or belief is forced or demanded in Epsilon Eridani. There is a free choice of studies given, and Epsilonians are able to follow their particular interests and passions. Everyone thrives and enjoys learning because they love to learn and they're not interested in being driven by fear, control, or force. When you've finished with your study you're encouraged to visit the astonishing Flower Library, which looks more like a designer garden than a library as we know libraries to be on Earth.

The first thing that grabs your attention is the variety of exotic flowers found there. They come in all shades of pink. You will see other colors, but pink is predominant. They reminded me of orchids except that one flower petal is longer and more pronounced than the others.

When you are beside these flowers you can sit, relax, and connect with their flower essence. You will make soul-to-soul connections and you may download all the information you require. This can be compared to downloading your favorite song onto your MP3 player. The only difference is that the flower is the source, and your heart (your soul) is the receiver of your new, fabulous MP3 track.

Epsilon Eridani starseeds are allowed to meditate and access this library of knowledge from their Earth base. This place is for you to use. You have earned access to it a long time ago. You can meditate here, calling for your guide and asking him or her to guide you into this magical garden on Erza.

Imagine walking through arched garden gates and walking toward the pink flowers. Walk to the one you feel drawn to the most. Now imagine that your soul light (energy in your chest) is growing bigger and brighter, and while this is happening the pink flower has a beautiful glow shimmering around it. Imagine these two lights gently merging together, becoming one. Then ask a question and listen for the answer, which may be in spoken words that you easily understand. Or perhaps you may experience an energy flow in your body. You may even see pictures in your mind.

Do not close yourself off to any experience or expectations. Accept with gratitude what you receive, and after your meditation, write down your experience. Remember, it may not make sense right away, but you may very well understand it later on. When you are done, ask your guide to take you back and do not forget to express your gratitude.

ENERGY POWER CENTER (EPC)

The Epsilon Eridani EPC can be located between the fourth and fifth chakras. This center is called the compassion chakra. You can experience this center as though the fourth and fifth chakras were merged together. Their energy is combined and the color is teal.

The compassionate chakra is the most sensitive center for Epsilonian starseeds. It is a place where they receive energy and send energy out. Epsilonian starseeds who have merged DNA with other star nations will have additional EPCs in their body. Depending on circumstances one center may feel stronger than the other. To better understand EPCs, when there is more than one it is like being right-handed and left-handed at the same time. With practice, you can learn to be both and use the associated skills as you need them. Andromedans have an EPC in their third chakra while Sirians have theirs in their sixth chakra.

ERIDANIAN STARSEEDS ON EARTH

There are many starseeds who incarnated on Earth with Epsilonians' DNA. Epsilon Eridani starseeds have a single DNA or merged DNA of different kinds, typically from Sirius or Andromeda. Since it is still not common to hear much about Eridanian starseeds, they may feel like they belong to Andromeda or Sirius, but there is a slight difference in their energy.

Those who've incarnated here on Earth with Epsilon Eridani DNA have a strong inner need for the truth. They feel like they have to search for answers and uncover lies, cover ups, and misleading information. Yet in the beginning of their journey they may have many fears that prevent them from being who they really are. Every fear they experience is connected to their past Earth lives, and not from experiences they had before incarnating on Earth. At first these fears act to protect Epsilon Eridanians from blindly jumping into their life's calling before they start to understand themselves and feel comfortable with who they are. Quite often they have been ridiculed and mistreated in the past and during past lives for voicing their opinion or for trying to uncover the truth. They carry wounded energy because other people did not believe them. Eventually they come to realize that their truth-seeking endeavors are valid and that others are at fault for not believing in them. Their challenge is to learn to hold back their judgement and respect other people's beliefs, and their choices.

Since they are such beautiful beings with pure souls, they often do not fight to prove that they are correct because fear often blinds the mind and, sadly, they surrender with hurt feelings. They hold their sadness inside so as not to upset anyone else. They feel angry but hide it well. This is sad because Epsilonian starseeds are extremely smart, kind, funny, and outgoing when they are feeling good about themselves.

Their gentle soul has a hard time dealing with any kind of physical brutality. Like the Pleiadians, they are inclined to attract abuse on all levels (sexual, emotional, and physical), and in this lifetime as well as past lifetimes they are typically born into difficult families. This brings trauma to their soul energy, and they have a hard time understanding why people choose to harm each other, which is unknown in their home world.

Epsilonian starseeds may appear as fragile souls, a little lost and withdrawn from other people when they don't feel supported. Giving comes naturally from their heart and they do not expect much back. Often other people notice this and take advantage of them. Their life pattern is often one of victim energy until they fully awaken and rise above all the obstacles that confront them and start learning who they are and what they can do. One of the first lessons could be facing their fears and breaking that old pattern. Typically thoughts of *I have done something wrong and I do not believe in myself* and/or *the whole world makes me upset because they do not see life as I see it* might plague them. Embracing a self-observing journey, of *who am I,* in a human body could be the best way for Epsilonian starseeds to learn all about the energy, inner strength, and courage that they have.

I have met Epsilonian starseeds who have nice healthy bodies. They dress according to the latest fashions and they enjoy the latest gadgets and trying new things. And I have also met those who carried extra weight. However, I sensed that the weight was just something for them to hide behind, something to protect them and keep them safe from all the abuse and suffering they endured on Earth. They are highly empathetic, sensitive, and receptive to negative energy, which can bring them a lot of insecurity and fear of the unknown. Feeling safe is one thing these starseeds have a problem with until they work through it.

Epsilonians are good listeners, and when they speak, they speak from the heart. Once they awaken their energy and cross the threshold of fears they will stand up for your rights. They will defend the truth and negotiate the best possible outcome for your situation. These are the people to have on your side. They try to avoid physical conflict as much as they can. If they find themselves in a fight they attempt to talk their opponent out of it with logic that comes from the heart.

To strangers, Epsilon Eridani starseeds may appear strict and reserved. In close circles of family and friends, however, they laugh and tell jokes and generally feel very comfortable. When you are around them you may notice they seem like they come from some sort of elite group, yet they never make you feel they are above you. They always treat others with respect, love, and dignity.

Epsilonian starseeds usually attract people with emotional problems. Needy people sense their compassionate energy and are unconsciously attracted to them. They are a magnet to those who may be in need of a mediator, an adviser, or those who need someone to uncover the truth for them. They also attract psychic vampires. These are people who just take or drain their energy. Since they have a hard time saying no and setting boundaries, this may be a great challenge for them.

When Epsilon Eridani starseeds feel passionate about what they do, they naturally vibrate their healing energy through their voice, which is their EPC. They do this unconsciously before their awakening and then get amazingly good at it once they figure out it's their gift.

Epsilon Eridani starseeds make great social workers, counselors, healers, writers (since they are good with words), investigators, lawyers, officers, negotiators, mediators, peacemakers, and scientists.

Many Epsilon Eridani starseeds like to express their feelings through art and create healing art pieces that emanate the energy they have put into them while creating them.

PRACTICES FOR ERIDANIAN STARSEEDS

✦ **Problem solving** comes naturally to Epsilonian starseeds, who are masters at harnessing wisdom in their hearts to peacefully resolve problems. Bring your awareness to any problem, issue, or conflict you may be pondering. It could be of any nature: a relationship, the kind of medication you are taking, or a change of occupation for instance, but focus on only one issue or problem at a time. Ask to be connected to the core energy of the problem. Feel it like a golden sphere in your heart chakra, slowly spinning in a clockwise motion. With each spin this golden sphere collects more information about the problem from your whole energetic imprint. Let go of your personal wants and needs regarding the outcome; just surrender and let the sphere spin until it stops. Once it stops, this sphere will project itself as a set of stars in front of you. Each problem often has several factors. Each factor is represented by a star, and you can intuitively feel or see what star quality it has: that of a dying star, a new star, or a bright star. Reach for the dying star and with love bring it into your heart chakra and let the wisdom of your starseed heart show you truth with compassion about what is ending, what needs change, and what you are holding on to in false illusion because you may be afraid. Once you understand this, let all feelings dissolve and bring in a new star. This star holds high potential for your future. Allow your starseed heart to show you the truth clearly and to receive guidance for the best resolution for everyone involved. Let it all dissolve and then bring in your bright star. Allow your starseed heart to show you the truth about yourself at the moment. Remember, there is no judgment, just plain truth. Knowledge like this will allow you to make changes without unnecessary conflicts. When you find yourself in chaos, focus on your heart and ask to be guided by the bright morning star, which symbolizes divine energy, wisdom, and love.

✦ **Connecting with the remarkable power of water** is another natural outlet for Eridanians. Oceans, rivers, streams, lakes, and waterfalls can greatly assist in uplifting your energy. Throughout history, mankind has benefitted from the transformative qualities of water. Just being near it has been shown to make us happier, healthier, and more relaxed. With such a positive impact on our physical, mental, and emotional well-being, consider strolling by the shore or wading in a stream when you can. Water is truly mystical—it transforms when exposed to words, sounds, and intentions (see the research of Dr. Masuru Emoto). Its strong energy field is further enhanced by rushing streams, waves, and waterfalls, and its high vibration can raise your own vibrational level.

+ **Boosting the benefits of swimming** is also advantageous to Eridanians. It's no secret that swimming is a profoundly healthy form of exercise, and by adding visualizations and intentions, it can become so much more. In addition to connecting with the power of water, the rhythmic motion of swimming (and breathing) calms the mind, soothes the nervous system, and helps to reduce the noise of our internal dialogue. One can transform a pool, lake, or ocean into a sanctuary in which to experience transcendent and meditative states. When swimming, try this practice: First, bring your complete attention to your body, noticing your heartbeat, the movement of your muscles, and the feeling of water on your skin. Then envision the water as liquid divine energy that surrounds and moves through you. Intuitively decide which aspects of your body, mind, and spirit to focus on. For instance, you might picture energy renewing your cells and organs, or removing emotional trauma, or clearing and recharging your aura. This restorative practice can greatly enhance your overall well-being.

+ **Visiting the beach, nature, and walking barefoot** (page 33 in Andromeda)

+ **Connecting with trees and other plants and creating your garden** (page 74 in Centaurus)

+ **Connecting with crystals** (page 74 in Centaurus)

MEDITATION
✳ Circle and Triangle Cleansing to Attain Clarity ✳

This cleansing was shown to me by Epsilon Eridani beings. If you are not an Epsilonian starseed, you still can use this wonderful cleansing meditation. It works for everyone. Just call for your guides and proceed as follows.

Find a quiet place and put on soothing music or light a few candles.

Take a few deep breaths in and out. Calm and empty your mind.

Now call for your Epsilon Eridani guide and ask for his or her assistance.

Imagine small geometric shapes, circles, and triangles. Imagine as many as you like. The circles and triangles will be a mix of a red and a deep-blue color. I like to call them "energy sponges." It doesn't matter which one is which; you can combine them as much as you like. Go with your intuition. These energy sponges will travel through your whole energy system, cleansing your chakras and aura and sponging up all the energy that no longer serves you in a positive way. They will work in a pattern of swiping from side to side. Then they will turn around in a circle and move upward in the body.

Imagine that the energy sponges are entering your Earth star chakra, which is about a foot below your feet. Feel or imagine them moving in a fast swiping motion from side to side in your chakra, expanding beyond the chakra and swiping your aura as well, and then turning in one full circle before moving upward.

Next visualize these energy sponges entering through your feet and moving upward to your calves and thighs before entering your base chakra.

The sponges swipe through your chakra horizontally, reaching the sides of your aura and then turn in a full circle before they move up from your root chakra to the sacral chakra.

Repeat the same action with the solar plexus, heart, and

throat chakras, swiping and sponging all the energy that is no longer needed from your chakras and aura.

When you finish with your throat chakra, these triangle and circle sponges will leave through your throat chakra and will stay in your aura to cleanse the aura around your brow and crown chakras.

When completed, these sponges will leave through the upper chakras above your head. They will finish the cleansing until they reach your soul star chakra, and then they will close your energy.

This cleansing is designed to clean the body and stimulate the mind. You do not have to do anything about cleaning your sponges. They will return back to their home world, Epsilon Eridani, and will be cleaned by your guides. You can call upon them whenever you need a cleansing of the body and clarity of mind. After this deep cleansing, imagine that your aura is sealed in a beautiful golden color for protection. Always express gratitude to your guides for working with you.

6

Lyra

Lyra is a small constellation that is bordered by the Dragon Draco, the Greek hero Hercules, Vulpecula (the Fox), and Cygnus (the Swan).

THE LYRAN BEINGS

Inhabitants of the Lyran star nation closely resemble humans in terms of our looks. They are older than Pleiadians, Sirians, or other star nations that we are currently connected with. In many of Earth's ancient texts Lyrans are referred to as Anunnaki. They would like us to understand that there is more information that we do not know.

I was trying to summarize information about these beings before realizing that sharing a channeled story would be the best way to represent them. *The Book of Missings* was shown to me in a lucid dream; this is the first story that the Lyrans would like me to share with you.

We, the Lyrans, resemble human beings. You may say that our origins are very close to your origins. We have been seeded, same as you, by other more developed star nations, and one day you may continue in this pattern.

There is a pattern, let's call it a cycle, a galactic/universal cycle that may be hard to comprehend. We will share our story with you, from the time leading to our home destruction when we were advanced and could utilize futuristic technology.

Our planet had been beautiful and pristine like yours. However, the other extraterrestrial civilizations in the galaxy were not a secret to us like they are to you. Everyone knew they existed—it was common knowledge. As on Earth, where different continents and people living in Africa, Europe, and Asia connect and communicate, we were connected with beings who were thriving in Centaurus, Sirius, the Pleiades, Andromeda, and other places in the universe. Life was normal and usually peaceful.

Problems blossomed when we finally acknowledged that our natural resources were running low. We had been warned many times before that this could happen. There had been red flags everywhere, yet we were ignorant. (Please note that the story we are telling is prior to the birth of your civilization. At that time, we were not much different than you are right now. Our population was growing and so was demand. We refused to be humble.)

Through the employment of artificial intelligence, our technology was developing and advancing at the speed of light. Believing that AI would solve our problems, we dismissed any other suggestions for change. We were close to being like the gods who had created us. This was such an exciting time, but sadly one that was fueled by a mind-centered drive. Of course, at that time we would not acknowledge this. The majority of us did not want to settle down with what we had or entertain alternative solutions. Power and technological advancement was what we desired. We wanted to dominate!

The Lyran star nation is composed of two unique races. Above we shared about the humanoid race that closely resembles the human look. The other is the feline-lion race that resembles the lion-cat-like beings. Our differences lie in our way of life. Where humanoid Lyrans are dominant in mind essence, feline-lion Lyrans are dominant in heart essence. Feline-lion Lyrans are sweet, compassionate beings, prioritizing the holistic approach to life. Let's compare them to spiritual people in your world. They could clearly see the future and believed that living from the heart was the best way to resolve our pressing issues. They tried to share that with us, but we would not listen, and naturally, they would not listen to our reasoning. Adamantly, they refused to accept life filled with advanced technology and AI to improve everyday life. Despite our obvious polarities, one living from the mind, another living from the heart (soul), we respected each other and lived in peace. If some of us desired to experience the others' way of life, we would be welcomed in those communities, without any judgment or need for assimilation.

All were natural leaders. It is encoded in our DNA, like survival and reproduction is encoded in yours. The more our intellect developed, the smarter we became and the more technology we craved. In the end, failure was unavoidable. Too afraid to embrace unconditional love and look for solutions, we put others of our kind on the path to destruction.

Looking back, our problem was that we lacked a heart-mind connection. When you live only from the heart (soul) or only from the mind, you create disharmony, because these two are twin flames in this universe. Eventually, we have learned that the best leaders' success derives from a soul-mind union.

One of our downfalls and greatest disconnections happened when we outsourced our mental capabilities to artificial intelligence. Naturally, it became smarter than we were. We falsely believed we were in control of it and followed the wrong advisers. Many things went wrong. Our world was destroyed because of our ill judgments and greed. We caused the malfunction of the system and could not stop the destruction that had begun.

Prior to the destruction many Lyrans, both humanoid and feline-lion, moved to Sirius and the Pleiades. It was part of a natural migration and was not done out of fear but rather out of a desire to learn and experience something new.

Before the destruction, we had to evacuate. It is shameful to admit that we were unable to evacuate everyone and prioritized those we thought were worthy of future survival—such as scientists, doctors, engineers, and developers, for instance. We abandoned regular folks. We boarded humongous spaceships and we negotiated with the

Council of Light. We pledged to be peaceful and aligned with the law of the Council of Light.

At this point, we thought we'd learned our lesson. Most of us were ready to change our lives and become more spiritual. We were offered several destinations in the universe in which to make our new home.

We underestimated life aboard the spaceships. Plainly, it became difficult. In a short time many of us grew angry, full of despair, and unnerved by an uncertain future. We were the leaders. We were used to comfortable houses with all kinds of luxuries, and now we found ourselves in small compartments of a ship with a tight schedule. We no longer had robots to do our work for us. Life was not easy anymore. We never thought this day would come. We were, as you say, very spoiled by our lifestyle.

While living in spaceships and negotiating peaceful settlements in other places we learned about the Pleiadians' project on Earth, called Lemuria. Lemuria was a peaceful civilization in a new world with full access to advanced technology but focused on spiritual practices and living from the heart (soul). Pleiadians shared with us findings about Earth's fascinating properties, including that the experiences of the senses and of the emotions could be heightened by being in a physical body.

We did not know much about emotions. We always knew what we wanted and we were not acquainted with moral consequences or emotional feelings. We constantly moved forward to attain our goals, believing that emotions were not an advantage, however unavoidable they were.

Pleiadians experimented with what can be called the science of the soul's energy. They knew that a Pleiadian existence was neither the beginning nor the end of the soul's journey. They thought that perhaps by observing emotions in the Earth's natural and primitive environment they would understand the beginning of our existence and where we were supposed to go next. Reaching levels of unconditional love was easy for them, but what was the next step?

After the initial study of Earth and her signature properties,

Pleiadians included a variety of star nations in their Lemurian project. This is where we came in—but not all of us, just a small fraction of us. We liked what we'd heard about Lemuria. Our original intent was to make Lemuria prosperous to everyone—harmonious and joyful. However, we underestimated the emotions that flooded us once we arrived on Earth. The feelings were new and shocking. Wars and home destruction had left tremendous scars on our souls that we didn't know how to deal with. Those who devoted time to spiritual growth saw the purity of the Earth and the heaven it could become. Those of an intellectual frame of mind felt a heightened urge for power and began to view Earth as an easy target. The Earth's energy had awakened suppressed anger over losing Lyra and partly clogged our logical mind. Lyrans thought, Well why not take Earth as ours?

Not all Lyrans had an intention to take over the Earth or knew about the plan to do so.

The cunning idea had to be preserved in deep secrecy and planned well ahead. Lyrans knew it would take time to dominate Earth. Lemuria was good, but Lyrans wanted more, rather than to just sit by the bonfire singing "Kumbaya." The Earth was rich with natural resources and bountiful with possibilities. Over time Atlantis was born. Andromedans, Sirians, and Pleiadians loved the creation of Atlantis, and Lyrans contributed to its growth.

The majority of us Lyrans did not foresee the upcoming deceit. We buried ourselves in the arts of healing, biology, and science. The effect of the magnetic field on the physical body and the superconsciousness was something we had never experienced before. We observed the split in subconsciousness, consciousness, and superconsciousness. In time, we designed many genetic experiments. Not everything went exactly as planned. We also became experts in cloning and programming our conscious mind within Earth's natural environment in order to adjust to life on Earth.

In Lyra we lived long lives. As a Lyran you could have control over your body and therefore over what your life would look like. Upon your birth in Lyra you would have full consciousness of your previous lives. Through your conscious mind you could easily access all of this information in your Akashic Records.

We Lyrans could also tamper with our consciousness. This was done for various reasons. For example, if you dedicated a certain amount of time to particular research, let's say solar energy, you could temporarily alter your conscious mind and neuropathic energy pathways (receivers of the information) to perceive only what was related to solar energy. This would give you a great focus on a particular topic. While consciously avoiding other distractions, you could be brilliant in the field of solar energy research. To explain this better, imagine a child prodigy who is born with autism. He could be a genius in one subject but lack skills in others. We can do this consciously by altering neuropathic pathways within a brain and reverse it back and forth. This knowledge allowed us to play God on Earth. We were masters of the genetic and bioengineering fields.

Lyrans thrived once again. By now you know that some of them wanted to dominate the Earth. They advocated for other star nations to join them on Earth. The split between spiritual beings from various star nations, as you call them in your words, now Children of the Law of One, and greedy beings from various star nations, the Sons of Belial, became tangible. The fight over power was no longer a secret.

In the meantime, Pleiadians found their answers and a pathway to God's house. No matter how good or bad anyone is, we all came from one source. Of course, the Sons of Belial refused to believe that. Pleiadians discerned that the journey back is through the soul, not through the stars. The answers are within, as they always have been. The illusions and charming opportunities clouded the vision to the House of God. Unfortunately, the original experiment on Earth created great soul suffering and produced an opportunity for various starseeds to literally become rogue and busy with their own manipulative agendas. Later on, when Pleiadians realized this, they pledged to be soul healers to all souls who embarked on a journey to the House of God.

We, the Lyrans who speak to you now, are the original spiritual beings who joined with the Children of the Law of One in Atlantis. We *believe that full knowledge of history is important. Many of you hold the energies of wounding and deception inside you. Perhaps you have been deceived by our kind or others; perhaps you worked on holding the balance and the light and felt defeated in the end. Perhaps you were part of the group who deceived others. It does not matter today.*

The nonjudgmental knowledge of what happened matters. Knowledge is power! This will lead to acceptance and forgiveness, and a breaking of the old cycle. We all have tremendous scars on our soul but by assisting each other we can collectively heal. We now understand that the Creator steered us toward the Earth to learn about unconditional love, compassion, and acceptance, not to dominate it.

We also want to share that we, and the other star nations, inhabited Venus, Mars, and Maldek. Maldek was destroyed not long before the final destruction of Atlantis. The remains of Maldek are an asteroid belt, but that is a story for another time.

Life on Earth was shaken with conflicts over the greedy domination. Crystal technology was used to harness natural powers without any consideration of the Earth's ability to produce it in the quantity desired by the Sons of Belial. Once again, the benefits of technology were greatly miscalculated in the same way they were on Lyra. Earth's core energy was abused and natural disasters were on the rise. The Children of the Law of One had foreseen the Atlantean predicament for some time prior to its destruction and tried to warn others without much success. Earth life was turning into a nightmare.

You may wonder why we did not call for help from the Council of Light, why forces had not been used to overturn the actions of the Sons of Belial. The answer is simple; the Earth had been a young planet. Maldek had just been destroyed (because one party wanted to take it over), and various dangerous experiments were happening on Mars. Our calling for help could have led to a major catastrophic event, including galactic war, with a risk of losing the Earth as you know it. The Earth's position and place in your solar system is important for the survival of many other beings in the universe. Atlantis was destroyed as a way to end the pervasive negativity and to allow various star beings to remain on Earth and teach others. If the Council of Light had interfered, a galactic war would have been unavoidable.

The destruction of Atlantis was inevitably coming. We knew we had to evacuate the area. We left the Sons of Belial to believe what they wanted. We had a choice to leave the Earth for good, without consequences or judgment, or to fully merge with the Children of the Law of One and correct many wrongdoings caused by various star beings from the universe. We knew we wanted to stay to assist in healing and learning. We also knew that this would be a long journey and that it would cause us pain, suffering, and disconnection. Spiritual Lyrans and Pleiadians negotiated with the Council of Light and secured the Earth as a free-will zone so that souls reincarnating here can learn, progress, and, when ready, access ancient knowledge and become like their ancestors.

After the destruction of Atlantis, the Children of the Law of One chose various lineages. Most well-known is the Egyptian lineage. Many left the land of Atlantis with heavy hearts, harboring feelings of failure and disappointment. They had a new mission: to teach all beings created on Earth to raise their consciousness and become like them. This would become quite a task—one that is still going on today. True teachers are born in each generation. In glimpses they remember the past and are allowed to teach by example. True teachers are leading their students to discover the truth for themselves.

It is only natural that some of the Sons of Belial had somehow survived the fatal incident as well. Slowly and steadily they rose again, making themselves gods. Over time, battles were fought between the dark and light forces. This pattern was created on Earth and has been repeating itself over and over until you (starseeds living on Earth) decide to change it.

THE HOME WORLD

The Lyrans' home world was destroyed. They settled in various places in the galaxy. The most well-known places were Andromeda, Sirius, the

Pleiades, and the most favorable: Centaurus. You may like to read about Centaurus to learn more about their new home world. Doing so will give you clues to your DNA and your genetic history.

ENERGY POWER CENTER (EPC)

The Lyran EPC is a little different from that of other star nations. There is no one specific area of the body in which it is located, as we have become accustomed to with other beings. The Lyran EPC creates a soft golden glow around their whole body, so perhaps we can say that their whole aura serves as an EPC. They can develop any abilities if they focus on them. Channeling skill is common for these starseeds as well as precognition or just intuitively knowing things. As with starseeds, if they want to become great at one ability or another, they need to focus on it and devote time to practicing that particular skill.

For Lyran hybrid starseeds, the Lyran EPC is usually the last to open. This is often a blessing in disguise in that they can focus first on one ability and one center at a time in order to avoid confusion. Lyrans are the oldest beings in relation to other star beings who are currently connecting with us. Currently all starseeds (Lyrans included) are born with a limited memory and a sensitive nervous system. A fully functioning EPC would be overwhelming to those who do not know how to work with this energy.

LYRAN STARSEEDS ON EARTH

Lyran starseeds are born to be leaders. When you speak with them you might notice a hint of authoritative energy emanating from them. Often they are unaware of that presence, which also vibrates with the serene and ancient energy of their soul. It is comforting to be in their company, even without saying a word.

To strangers they appear polite, amicable, and always professional. No matter what work position they hold, their high level of sophistication (not ego) gives you the impression that they are the CEO of the company. They are responsible, have confident self-esteem, and are organized for the most part. If their house or workplace gives the impression that something is out of order, it is just an illusion, as they know perfectly where everything is. As some may say, they are an organized disaster.

Usually, they have excellent taste in clothes and amenities. Simplicity and sophisticated design is frequently preferred by them rather than braggier flashy art or furniture. They do like elegant expensive things that blend in with their surroundings, but you will hardly notice them. Their homes carry the warmth of family and comfort.

Family bonds are very important to them. In close circles of family and friends they feel relaxed and are not afraid to show the loving, kind, and devoted side of their personalities. They are fun to be around and make you feel at ease and welcome. Some Lyran starseeds like to cook and some totally stay away from that task, leaving it up to their partner or their family. Despite their cooking preferences, they like to eat in a healthy way and generally take good care of their bodies. They have extensive knowledge of the benefits of particular foods, supplements, and exercise protocols.

Some Lyrans are not engaged in healthy lifestyles until after their awakening process. However, it is something that is in the back of their minds and high on their priority list. If they engage in self-destructive behavior such as drinking or using drugs, for instance, it is just a temporary phase in their life that typically doesn't last long.

They love to acquire new knowledge and pursue continuous education in anything that interests them. Decision-making comes naturally to Lyran starseeds because they can observe situations without emotional attachment. Sometimes they may appear cold and unfriendly, but once you get through their outside shield, which they created to protect themselves from possible judgment by others, they will become your best friend. They have sharp minds and honest hearts.

Lyran starseeds who have not gone through an awakening process may be stubborn and struggle with an ego that wants to dominate and always be right. It can bring them trouble when they are trying to convince others that their truth is correct. At times, they may even become unpleasant to be around. Frustration and unhappiness usually leads to an awakening moment and transformation.

Even though they are extremely intelligent and in many cases have a high level of Earth education, they sacrifice their own dreams and desires so their partner can pursue his or hers. They become the person behind the scenes and help their partner to succeed beyond his or her expectations. They never blame anyone for their personal choices in life, and fully embrace and accept the supportive role that they alone have chosen.

I believe that somewhere deep inside of them are hidden fears and memories of past, misused energy by their star kind, and on a subconscious level they are afraid to fully step into their starseed energy. To get past these unconscious blocks, they bury themselves in many projects such as volunteering with nonprofit organizations (some of them extremely successful and fascinating) to avoid their true calling: that of being a true spiritual teacher and leader.

Lyran starseeds are devoted spiritual beings. They enjoy meditating, energy healing, crystals, and studying various types of spiritual modalities. They are fascinated with religion and sometimes even join particular religions to be able to fully understand them. Their childhood is usually turbulent, but they will make you feel like it was great. Mistreatment, emotional abuse, or bullying during their early years does not traumatize them. They understand it because it helped shape them into who they are. Often during a difficult time they may be experiencing, at least one family member adores them and loves them and that is all they need for balance to survive in this place we call Earth. They learn to hold on to good events and release unhappy ones.

Forgiveness is a big lesson for them in this lifetime—forgiveness of themselves and others. Time and again, life's lessons throw all kinds of rocks in their path, often giving them reasons to work on forgiveness. This could be prevented by conscious, forgiveness energy work. When they consciously embark on a forgiveness journey, the energy works its magic all the way back to their ancestral lines and brings healing on a broader scale to everyone involved.

Lyran starseeds seek solitude, and long hours alone are appreciated. They are never bored. They like to read or watch nonstressful television shows. They love any kind of art and regularly create art of their own as this gives them the solitude they need.

From my connection with Lyran starseeds and observing what they choose for a professional career, a great occupation would be teaching (any topic), school principal, artist, writer, business owner (because of their organizational skills), researcher, scientist, engineer, motivational speaker, life coach, or news reporter. They literally can do anything and engage in any workplace that brings them comfort and happiness.

THE ART OF FORGIVENESS

One of the major lessons that you come to Earth to learn is forgiveness. We, the Lights of the Universe, understand how hard it is to forgive all wrongdoings that occur in your Earth life.

We are assisting you to feel love in your heart, versus the dark side putting emphasis on the negative emotional senses that are heightened in Earth's realm. Negative energy is easier to sense than positive because it's composed of lower vibrations. It wants to enslave you in a 3D reality. In order to be incarnated, the majority of you have had to lower your vibration. This causes you to be more susceptive to negative energy until you learn how to raise your vibration once again.

Sometimes it's difficult to disassociate from your hurt and look at it with an objective perspective. You may think that you are lonely, that no one understands you, that God/Source/the Universe has abandoned you and left you to suffer. But that is not correct. Please know in your heart that God has never abandoned you and know in your heart that the assistance you need can be invoked by your will and your spoken words.

The art of forgiveness, as we call it, has to originate from your heart (your soul) instead of your mind.

In the following meditation you will be guided to forgive others as well as forgive yourself. Forgiveness needs to go both ways. You may ask why.

It does not matter if you are the victim or the perpetrator. Send the forgiveness to the opposite side and to yourself to create a balance. This enables you to be free.

The majority of people who become a victim (no matter the circumstances) believe it's their fault: if they hadn't been at a particular place at a particular time, if they'd only behaved better (children especially are prone to believe this), if they could only work harder, and so on and so forth; these thoughts and others are prone to fill their minds.

Every victim is filled with shame and guilt. If you are a victim, in order to be able to forgive, you need to first accept that the way things have turned out is not your fault. You need to forgive yourself for being in that situation. You need to forgive yourself for feeling ashamed, guilty, and most probably wishing very bad things to happen to the one who hurt you. This is natural. An interesting fact is that when the perpetrator becomes conscious of his or her actions, they are filled with the same energy of shame and guilt that can eat you alive.

All victims and consciously aware perpetrators (who are in the phase of consciously regretting their actions) hide their feelings of fear inside and unconsciously give up their personal power. As a result their inner soul light grows dim. This shame/guilt energy affects not only the physical body, but the soul as well. This particular energy can travel with you from incarnation to incarnation. Both victims and perpetrators are scared to be whole again. What if someone violates their energy again? What if they abuse their power again? Sadly, some souls are so lost that they do not even know or remember how to be whole, or even where to begin on the path to reclaiming their wholeness.

When you forgive yourself and others you take your power back! You collect pieces of your soul that had been taken away from you, or that you had given away!

Consciously allowing yourself to heal while setting judgment aside is a big step. No one can do that for you because it would be against your free will. You can get assistance in many forms, but the final step of allowing yourself to take your power back, to forgive, is yours.

PRACTICES FOR LYRAN STARSEEDS

+ **Strengthening your aura,** which for Lyrans serves as their EPC, can be very beneficial for Lyrans. When it is strong and balanced it has a soft golden glow, and Lyran starseeds can easily, with practice, develop healing their energetic and psychic abilities. The ability to be a clear channel is one of the dominant traits of these starseeds. Their aura has seven layers, and each layer has a particular energy and purpose. Strengthen your aura with a simple exercise, beginning with your first chakra. Tune in to the red spinning energy of the first chakra. Feel what this center means to you and how it feels, what is working for you and what is not. This will give you a clue what you need to work on. Next, extend this red energy from inside, out of your body, building a strong first layer of aura. You can think of an eggshell with seven layers; this is your first inner layer. Move into your second chakra, which is orange, and repeat the same action until you finish with your seventh chakra, which is violet. When you start this practice, focus on what you feel in each layer, what is working for you, and what needs to change. Your abilities will open only when you understand yourself and transform yourself into a better version of you. When you are done with the seven layers, imagine golden energy rising from Earth and also coming down from the universe, creating a soft golden glow that seals your aura. This is your cocoon, made of unconditional love and filled with universal wisdom. Everything you need to develop your abilities is within you.
+ **Nurturing creativity** helps Lyrans to express themselves. Creativity is about imagining, exploring, and letting ideas and intuition flow freely. Creating art helps to put us in touch with our emotions, increasing self-awareness. Choose a type of art that appeals to you,

such as watercoloring, sketching, painting, or crafting. To guide you, find lessons and instructional videos online or join a local art class. Consider letting your artwork branch into other areas of your life. For example, make a journal that combines art with writing about your thoughts and dreams. Or create a collage with pictures and drawings that reflect specific goals. (This is a great technique for enhancing the manifesting process.)

+ **Studying various spiritual and religious traditions** to create a belief system that works for you is also a good idea. Religions and schools of spiritual thought are pathways to the Divine. Just as there are many different paths up a mountain that all reach the same peak, the right path to God is the one that resonates with you. Some of the wonderful attributes that many spiritual traditions share are compassion, unconditional love, forgiveness, and kindness. When designing the elements of your spiritual practice, search for prayers and invocations that touch your soul, and look for sacred texts, books, and wisdom teachings that inspire you. You might also bring the power of ritual to your practice. Celebrate the cycles of the year (such as the summer and winter solstices) and meditate using sacred symbols or mantras. Making your spiritual tradition part of your daily life can bring lasting tranquility and an expanded awareness of divine guidance.

+ **Visiting the beach, nature, and walking barefoot** (page 33 in Andromeda)

+ **Connecting with trees and other plants and creating your garden** (page 74 in Centaurus)

+ **Connecting with crystals** (page 74 in Centaurus)

MEDITATION
✳ The Art of Forgiveness ✳

Find a quiet place and make yourself comfortable.

You can close your eyes or keep them open, whichever you prefer. Take a deep breath in and exhale all the air out.

Take another deep breath in, hold it in for about three seconds, and then exhale all the air out. Take one more deep breath in, hold the air in for three seconds, and exhale all the air out.

Invite your guides, angels, archangels, God, Creator, Jesus, or your loved ones from the other side (everyone you believe in), to assist you in forgiving yourself and others. You can say in your mind or out loud: "I ask you and thank you (state the name of the divine helper you'd like to call in for assistance) for joining me today and assisting me in learning the art of forgiveness."

Imagine a beautiful golden light forming just above your head. Its energy is warm and soothing. The golden light is shining down upon you and you feel calm and peaceful. It makes you feel safe. Now imagine that this golden light is slowly coming down and sur-rounding you, expanding your aura. You can breathe this golden energy in and out and feel your whole being with it. The Lights of the Universe, assisted by your guides, created this golden light energy for your healing.

Take a deep breath in and exhale. Bring your awareness into your chest, then into your heart chakra. This is where your soul sits. Think of the time you got hurt. Recall the unhappy event as vividly as you can. It is okay to feel it strongly—as if it has just happened. Now, think of the person or people connected to this event. Be specific.

Put both of your hands on your heart chakra. Feel your heart-beat. Feel your soul. Take a moment to feel you, the essence of your being. Now think with your heart, forgiving the person or people who have caused your unhappiness. Say out loud: "I am sending forgiveness to the soul of (name the person) for (state what happened) to me. I forgive you and I am sending love and light to you."

Take a deep breath in and release all the air out.

Now say out loud: "I am sending forgiveness to myself, to my own soul for feeling ashamed, guilty, and blaming myself for what happened. I forgive myself and I am sending love and light to myself."

Take a deep breath in and release all the air out.

Now say out loud with great meaning: "I ask and thank you for the pieces of my soul that I have given away, to be returned back to me now!"

Leave your left hand on your heart and move your right hand onto your throat chakra. Once again, think about the same situation and the same person or people. The energy of your heart will connect with your voice and expression. This will enable you to find your voice and will give you inner strength.

Now feel within your heart that you have forgiven the person or people who caused you unhappiness and feel that you have the power to speak about it without feeling bad.

Say out loud: "I am sending forgiveness to the soul of (name the person) for (state what happened) to me. I forgive you and I am sending love and light to you." Take a deep breath in and release all the air out.

Now say out loud: "I am sending forgiveness to myself, to my own soul for feeling ashamed, guilty, and blaming myself for what happened. I forgive myself and I am sending love and light to myself."

Take a deep breath in and release all the air out.

Now say out loud with great meaning: "I ask and thank you for the pieces of my soul that I have given away, to be returned back to me now!"

Leave your left hand on your heart and move your right hand onto your sixth chakra, covering your brows. Once again, think about the same situation and the same person or people. The energy of your heart will connect consciously with that of your mind. This will enable you to consciously cleanse your mind and let go of unhappy thoughts. "I am sending forgiveness to the soul of (name the person) for (state what happened) to me. I forgive you and I am sending love and light to you."

Take a deep breath in and release all the air out.

Now say out loud: "I am sending forgiveness to myself, to

my own soul for feeling ashamed, guilty, and blaming myself for what happened. I forgive myself and I am sending love and light to myself."

Take a deep breath in and release all the air out.

Now say out loud with great meaning: "I ask and thank you for the pieces of my soul that I have given away, to be returned back to me now!"

Put your hands back on your heart and send love to yourself. Think of your loved ones and your guides, think of us, the Lights of the Universe. We, the Lights of the Universe, are here with you at this moment. Feel the love we are sending you right now. Feel love energy expanding in your heart, your soul. Feel that you are one with the universe and feel that you are a being of light and connected with everything and everyone that is.

When you feel ready, express your gratitude to everyone who has assisted in your healing.

Stretch your arms, stretch your legs, and come back to your body. Notice how different you feel.

Afterword

This starseed guide was written with the purpose of reminding you of the past and awakening the ancient being within your soul, so that you may realize that you are much more than just a body made of flesh and bones. You are a powerful being of light, a member of the vast stellar family, having a human experience.

The Pleiadian star nation is one of the most frequently discussed star nations that we know of. Pleiadians are soul healers and so are their starseeds on Earth. They are our ancestors, teachers, and loving companions throughout our lives. They're teaching us that in the universe there are many others like them who have the highest degree of beneficial interest in us and for the Earth.

LIVING WITH THE PLEIADIANS: MY STORY

The short version of how I met the Pleiadians is that they have always been with me. However, my journey of becoming consciously aware of them and accepting that they are part of my reality—my soul family, my friends, and my guides—involves a much more detailed story. I invite you to walk with me through my past and into the present as I share that story with you.

Our past is something that shapes us into who we are today. We have a choice to relate to the past with sadness and anger, or with forgiveness and love. I hope that in the same way that I was able to find my true self, you will be encouraged to embark on a journey of self-discovery, forgiveness, and love.

Ever since I can remember, I have always felt different from others. I felt like I didn't fit in, like I was born in the wrong place. I even felt as if I was adopted, which of course wasn't true. I was born in Czechoslovakia and grew up in the small city of Jesenik (Freiwaldau), which is nestled in the hills of north Moravia. Growing up with a dysfunctional childhood that was further complicated by the energy of difficult past lives caused me to develop a victim personality. I was eager to please everyone, felt ashamed and guilty on an everyday basis, and fear ruled my life. If I was not scared, I was angry, yet I buried my anger deep inside because being angry, in my mind, meant that I was a bad person. I hid all my problems and emotions, and instead pretended to have the normal, ordinary life that was expected of me.

I spent a great deal of my childhood at my grandparents' home in the country, playing with farm animals, climbing trees, exploring the forest, and pretending that I lived somewhere far in the past where life was simply beautiful.

AWAKENING

My first conscious spiritual journey began with electricity. I electrocuted myself when I was around one-and-a-half years old, and it was not an accident. Strangely, I recall planning to do this with excitement, which I think is a bit odd for a toddler. I remember walking into our hallway and sensing energy in the walls with my tiny hands. I could feel an electric current running horizontally in the wall.

My mother was an avid knitter, and she had a basketful of metal needles. While she was busy I took two knitting needles and stuck them both in the electrical outlet. I received a huge electric shock that knocked me unconscious. I can remember looking at myself from above my body and seeing my worried mother scoop me up and carry me to the sofa. She was soothing me with her voice and a pacifier.

It took a few minutes for me to regain consciousness, and when I did, I sneaked off the sofa and did it once more. This time my mother became so angry with me that I never attempted it again. I suppose it was my soul's way of keeping my spiritual door open, which normally closes as a child grows older.

In the years to come, in my dreams and daydreams I would journey in the universe, seeing remarkable mandalas in breathtaking colors and feeling unconditional love. I wished I could be in that space all the time. However, with the good aspects of this ability also came the bad. I could sense earthbound spirits and entities of a low vibration. I had no name for that back then, I just felt very uncomfortable and frightened about something I couldn't explain. I sensed the presence of invisible people looking at me, trying to touch me or get my attention. I would refuse to go to some places or into some rooms, fearing that someone or something might harm me. No one understood what was happening to me, and I could not understand it myself. There are some bad-energy entities out there in the universe, but the most frightening experiences came from some of the living human beings I met. I could feel other people's emotions and intentions as if they were my own. Some of these encounters would paralyze me with fear for the next three decades of my life.

A GREAT DARKNESS

Shortly after my experiment with electricity, my mother introduced me to my soon-to-be stepfather. A tall, charming, handsome man smiled at me and I perceived a great darkness in him. I was filled with uneasiness and fear. Unfortunately, he proved to be a living nightmare for many years to come. His actions instilled other levels of fear within me: fear of the night, fear of the darkness, and fear of the death of those I loved the most. He was a very troubled soul who has long since passed away. I would like to state here as I am writing the story of my life today, that I no longer harbor any bitterness or resentment toward him. One of my big life lessons was to forgive him. I also forgave my mother, realizing that she'd tried to do the best for us kids. After forgiving him, I embraced him in universal love; I am capable of loving him despite all the things he'd done to us.

The human psyche is fragile and shapes us into someone we may not want to be. You can easily become a victim, and some people become an oppressor, living that life unconsciously and making the lives of others extremely painful. However, if you can embark on a path of healing, you no longer have to be a puppet of your emotions. You can rediscover yourself and be who you want to be, consciously choosing a path of authentic empowerment. Everyone can change. We can all heal our soul; we can forgive and love, and that is a lesson I learned from him.

You may wonder why the Pleiadians did not interfere in this dark scenario. Many people who have shared their own life struggles with me become angry about why this or that happened, and they wonder why their guides or God did not intervene and protect them. The truth is that our soul family is always there. They cannot interfere with physical actions, but they can supply us with the energy needed so that we may make constructive changes in our lives. We all have within us a spark of God and we carry the DNA of our extraterrestrial family. Through our suffering we are awakening our abilities and our memories and rising up into our own soul power. We are born into a world of fears and we are learning to transform those fears into love. We are becoming God-like, which in essence is what we truly are.

The Pleiadians are teaching us. It is all up to us to make changes in our lives. The Pleiadians would come to me in my dreams and show me love. They would guide me to the local library where I found love in books and could live through the stories I read. What I read has been a gift they gave me, opening so many doors for me and enabling me to escape into my imagination. The next gift I received was a love of nature. I would walk by the trees and could feel them talking to me, giving me the strength to persevere through difficult times. Later on, the Pleiadians guided me to start writing my own journal.

Occasionally anxiety and panic attacks would keep me up at night. I was guided to articles on mental health and psychology with a full explanation about panic attacks—how they happen, how long they last, and that, while being quite unpleasant, they aren't fatal. I was only about twelve years old, and I didn't know the term *panic attack,* but by reading about symptoms I could diagnose and help myself. On so many occasions during those years, I intuitively felt the guidance of the Pleiadians. Again, they have always been there, but they could not physically interfere. This is a rule, a cosmic law.

THE SPACESHIP

I was about three years old when I began to draw (in my child's mind) elaborate blueprints of a spaceship. We had an old-fashioned sofa in the living room that had a solid wood bottom. Since I was banned from coloring after an episode of expressing my artistic skills on our living room wall, I would hide under the sofa and create my masterpiece down there on the bottom of the sofa. I actually found it comforting, relaxing, and safe. It was a perfect home for my soul. I felt like I was on the spaceship I was drawing and, for the record, my job was to make a draft of it. I remember the oval shape of the ship and numerous rooms separated by thin material that made up the walls.

Great emphasis was placed on the design of each room (its shape, either square or triangular), and on the sequence of the rooms. For example, you would not put the kitchen next to the room where surgeries were performed. I recall feeling the presence of many people on that ship; they closely resembled the human race. I thought the ship was blue, but I made all the drawings in red. Back then I knew nothing of UFOs or the Pleiadians. One day, about three years later, I came home from school and our old sofa had been replaced with a brand-new one. I was sad, but life went on.

A MESSAGE FROM THE OTHER SIDE

My grandfather was the most influential man in my life. He passed away when I was eighteen years old. Throughout his life my whole family teased him, saying that he loved me so much that he wouldn't die without seeing me one last time. Sadly, this turned out to be true. Unexpectedly, he had a stroke and fell into a coma, and he passed away a day after I came to see him. We all believed he moved his hand a tiny bit to wave goodbye to us; he knew we were there. I was heartbroken and lost—we all were.

A few days after the funeral I had my first lucid dream. I was sleeping in the kitchen on the sofa and he sat at our dinner table. He told me not to be scared and sad anymore. He said that now he lived in America and that one day I would be living there too. He told me not to be afraid of going there, that I would find my happiness there. Then he stood up and I saw him walk through the window and then down the street. He turned a little and with a smile he waved his final goodbye, as if to say, "See you in America!" and then I woke up. I could still feel his presence in the room for a moment, then it was gone.

I sat alone in the silent darkness. My heart raced and I felt such fear (wondering if my grandfather had really just talked to me) that I slept in my sister's room that night. When morning came I was embarrassed, so I casually joked about having spent the night in her room, but without question, spirits and energies still alarmed me at that point.

I told my mother about the dream, but it sounded like nonsense. My grandfather was supposed to be in heaven. And regarding me living in the States, being safe and happy where I was, at eighteen I had no desire or opportunity to move there—it seemed too far away. After that experience I worked hard to shut down my ability to feel spirits by pretending there was nothing out there and telling myself that I was simply a jumpy, fearful person who did not like to be alone. My mother would communicate with spirits on occasion as well, but she had no real answers or explanations either.

HOPING FOR A NORMAL LIFE

Throughout my teenage years I struggled to define my own identity, and I was experiencing the spiral of suffering that comes from having a victim mindset. My beautiful dreams stopped. I no longer wanted to read, and my "victim ego" eagerly created its own identity and acted up on occasion. I believed that no one understood me, and there was no one like me, or so I thought. I also started drinking alcohol to soothe my emotional pain and to help me escape from my thoughts. I wondered if all the energy and the presence of the spirits that I could sense were there just to produce more chaos in my life. I thought it could possibly be my karma; little did I know that I was cocreating the chaos with my own energetic distress. Where were the Pleiadians during this time? They patiently waited until I got all of this out of my system.

I met my first husband when I was nineteen years old, and we married shortly thereafter. I was determined to have a normal life, but in reality my life was far from typical. My husband was twenty years older than me and quite troubled by his own life circumstances, but I was in love. Our move to the States came as a sudden opportunity, and in a matter of three months in 1998 we were on an airplane heading for Boston. When we landed, I felt this beautiful energy of "I am home," and when the immigration officer said, "Welcome to America," I had to hold back tears of joy.

THE FIRST WAVE

My first wave of conscious awakening came two years later. My grandmother passed away suddenly, just as my grandfather had. I did not get to see her one last time. I could not travel back to Czechoslovakia and I felt extremely guilty about that. I would light candles for her and tried to talk to her. Little did I know that by doing this I unconsciously opened the spiritual door that I had closed after my grandfather's passing.

At this time I had big dreams. I wanted to be successful and have abundance, and I was willing to work hard to achieve that. I was working as an assistant manager at a fast-food restaurant. With my poor English I was thrilled when my boss hired me and told me that if I proved myself, maybe one day I could be a manager. I eagerly did all the jobs assigned and learned all the stations. I also learned to speak

English more fluently and eventually climbed my way up to a management position.

Then one day I woke up and felt as if the whole world was spinning around me. My energy awakening was starting to happen, and it felt so overwhelming that I worried it would shatter all of my hopes and dreams. I had a heightened sense of awareness, but along with it, the panic attacks and anxiety I experienced in childhood had returned, and they did not stop there. People often made me feel anxious now as well, because I felt their emotions and demands, and the noises from machines reverberated uncomfortably, with high-pitched, piercing sounds. Feeling totally confused, I wondered, *What will I do now?* I was young but my body had no energy, and I had no idea that what I was experiencing was the start of an intense energetic shift affecting my body, mind, and soul.

One evening as I drove home from work I had to pull over because my hands went numb, and I had an episode of profound anxiety. For the first time, I started to fully realize the extent of the stress and sadness in my life. I often had sleep deprivation and felt exhausted. I worked busy twelve-hour shifts and then came home to a depressed husband who did not work at the time and always pointed out my faults, and according to him I had a lot of them. Forced to take a few days off to rest, I felt I was in the midst of a major life crisis. Interestingly enough, it was my husband who suggested meditation and showed me how to connect with the restorative energy of trees. I would also sit on the beach, and I learned to stop my racing thoughts little by little to achieve moments of healing and tranquility. That was a lifesaver, and I returned to work being much more in control of my feelings.

I knew I had to take care of my nervous system and reduce my anxiety. If the ocean and trees could make me calm, then I could achieve that. I improved my eating habits and took supplements to strengthen my nervous system. Most of all, I learned to take care of my inner self, and I slowly started to work on building my feelings of worthiness. I realized I didn't need to please everyone all the time and that saying no is okay. I stopped volunteering to work on my days off, and I cut down on those long hectic work hours. I'd finally made the decision to prioritize my own well-being.

Eventually I changed jobs, working at a retail store in a more relaxed environment. The calmer work pace was just what I needed to rejuvenate my nervous system and give myself a break. Little did I know that there I unconsciously started to practice my psychic abilities. The Pleiadians were there with me! I would assist customers in picking out their window treatments, and many times they didn't know the size of their windows, yet it was like I could see through their eyes, allowing me to recommend the correct items. One day a friend and coworker commented about this, marveling at the fact that I somehow knew exactly what was needed. I'd never thought about that before—to me it felt like I just knew what they were looking for. During that time I also started to acknowledge that I could once again feel energy the way I'd been able to as a child.

It was all starting to come back to me.

AUTOMATIC WRITING

One day, when I was three months pregnant with my first child, my mother called to inform me that she had a feeling that my deceased grandfather wanted to talk to me. She had a message from his spirit for me that I should start communicating with him through automatic writing. I doubted that, but then curiosity won out. Skeptically, I tried it and my hand would start to scribble circles and a few words suggesting it was my grandfather communicating with me. Could that be? I missed my grandparents so much, but I wanted an affirmation that this was not just my imagination. My husband's mother had passed away before I could meet her, so I asked if she could give me some information that I did not know, and I received it. I was surprised and intrigued at the same time.

Then one day I saw the psychic John Edward on TV and thought that I could possibly help people connect with their loved ones. I started to read about other mediums and signed up for a class that would enable one to develop their psychic abilities. I could feel the energy, but when we were supposed to meet our guides, I could not make a connection. People in the class shared some amazing stories, but I couldn't relate and I was a bit disappointed.

ASTRAL TRAVEL

When pregnant I had a premonition of my daughter Eva's birth, which turned out to be valid. Sleep deprivation once again rattled my nervous system, and this time I began to astral travel. As soon as I would lie down I would see myself leaving my body, looking at my exhausted self. I would travel to my grandparents' house, where as a child I'd been able to rejuvenate my energy. This would scare me, but I didn't know how to stop it, and I needed the rest that traveling to my grandparents' house provided.

I became a stay-at-home mom and started reading more, and worked on steadily improving my English. Gathering up enough courage to tell a few people that I could sense spirits, I began to deliver messages I received from the other side. I never found it easy to tell anyone these messages; I always worried what they would think. I would get the words stuck in my throat and would blush horribly. At that point I wasn't sure if I was blessed or cursed with what I sensed and felt.

Two and half years after my daughter was born, our son Ethan arrived. On the first day we nicknamed him ET. I felt our little family was complete now, and I guess the Pleiadians were ready to consciously come back into my life. One day I met a new mom at our local children's playgroup, and I felt I had to ask her for a playdate. Even though she turned me down a few times, we eventually agreed to meet. I did not know why, but I was determined to meet this woman. Our kids played and we talked, and we realized we were both interested in spirituality. She loaned me the book *Opening to Channel* by Sanaya Roman and asked if I would read it and maybe we could discuss our experience. I was excited about this, so I read the book and started to do the energy exercises described in its chapters.

KENEAU ARRIVES

Then one day while I was washing dishes I sensed the presence of a male energy by my right side. I acknowledged it and suddenly I clearly heard in my head the name *Keneau*. Emotions swirled over my heart as if I had just heard from someone I hadn't seen in a very long time. The next thing I heard was the word *Pleiades*. At that moment I stopped what I was doing and had an ah-ha moment. Overwhelmed with emotion, I had to sit down, and I spontaneously started to speak what I now know is the Language of Light. The spoken words that I had no conscious recognition of brought waves of tears to my eyes, but they weren't tears of sadness; it was the joy of a beautiful reunion. I was certain I had finally connected with my guide, and this must be his language!

Just writing about it reminds me that I never questioned the fact that he spoke a language that no one could understand. In my heart, I just knew this was normal. After all, I'd seen a UFO twice as a child and my mother would joke that she talked to ETs, so it was not scary or strange to me. The energy I experienced cannot be described in words; it was a level of unconditional love that I had never felt before. After the moment was over, I wondered what or who *Pleiades* was. I read online the definition of the Seven Sisters star system, and my heart pounded in my chest.

Somehow I knew that what was happening to me was real. There was a moment where my life flashed in front of my eyes, and I knew that everything that had happened to me up to that point in life was fine, and that I would also be fine going forward. I knew I had to let go of blaming others for my life circumstances, and I had to release my fears. This was a tremendously insightful moment of clarity where everything was aligned with everything that is.

I began to meditate daily and started to communicate with Keneau through automatic writing. I could hold his frequency for about thirty seconds to one minute, and then it was gone. I was frustrated but I never gave up. Keneau would tell me that I was one of them, and I'd wonder how that could be—I am a human in this lifetime. He would speak in a philosophical way and would give me guidance, like suggesting that I should learn energy healing. It was always up to me whether I would follow the guidance or not. After Keneau suggested that I was a healer, I started to learn Reiki and energy routines as shared by Donna Eden in her book *Energy Medicine.* I learned that everything is energy and it doesn't matter if you practice healing or not; you need to have knowledge of energy to even begin to comprehend the unknown. Around the same time, I also had a lucid dream where someone audibly told me, "You are a soul healer!" Startled, I woke up, still hearing the words.

It took years of learning and giving healings, readings, and workshops, and slowly healing my own victim pattern and ego (which we all have), until several years ago when I consciously and profoundly understood that I am indeed a soul healer. I can connect to the soul and see its wounds and create conscious ah-ha moments of knowledge and insight to heal the soul and the body as well.

Each soul contains tremendous healing power within.

BATTLING LYME DISEASE

In 2008 I suddenly became ill. I was awfully tired and I developed a high fever, extreme headaches, and pains throughout my whole body. My neck seemed to be paralyzed. I knew this was not just the flu, and that something was seriously wrong. Since we had no medical insurance my husband decided he would cure me instead of going to see a doctor. He was very dominant in our relationship and I didn't have the will to argue. This lasted for almost a week, and I was getting steadily worse.

Then one night as I drifted off to sleep I escaped my pain-ridden body. I went to what I can only describe as the Crystal City. I saw temples and everything appeared to be made out of crystal. I am convinced this was not heaven, but it was the most beautiful place I had ever seen. Everything was a brilliantly luminous shade of white. The energy of the place cannot be described in words, and just saying that it radiated love or peace doesn't do it justice. There I heard spoken words that were like enchanted lyrics that rhymed. I wanted to stay there forever.

I don't remember seeing anyone, but I received a full awareness of what was going on with my physical body. Instantly I knew I had Lyme disease and that I needed to go to a doctor to get medical help. Yet I had no desire to go back to that body, so I asked if I could stay. At that moment, I was shown my two little children. Did I really want to stay? I knew I had to go back for them. They were the best thing that had ever happened to me.

Returning back into my body was brutal. Once I entered I felt extreme heaviness and pain, and realized how tired and diseased my body was. I knew that somehow I had to change this situation. When I fully awakened I had a surge of energy. It was like a miracle. I googled "signs of Lyme disease" and saw all of my symptoms listed. I knew that was what I had. My husband was not as convinced, but he was willing to listen. Angels were all around me that day.

My friend called me that morning to ask why I missed her kid's birthday party, and I told her about my symptoms. I told her that my husband did not want me to go to the doctor, and she said that if he didn't take me then she would, that day! She found me a free clinic that referred me to a hospital where I was diagnosed with Lyme disease. I received high doses of antibiotics for the next three months. That was just the beginning of my recovery. The pain eased, but my nervous system, my immune system, and my energy levels were shutting down. I was a walking zombie, but I knew I could not give up. I had kids, no other family in the States to help me, and I had to get better.

I wondered about the place I'd gone to when I connected with the Crystal City, or what others call "Shambala," the inner city inside the Earth. I had prayed for help, and someone answered my cry. However, they did not heal me; they gave me an energy boost and the knowledge of what I needed to do to heal myself. I started to understand why Keneau had been telling me that I was a healer, and why he suggested that I learn energy healing: it's because this knowledge literally saved my life.

I began to implement everything I had learned and worked on healing myself each day until I recovered. This experience was the beginning of me taking my power back. At this point I also knew I had to change my life, and I left my husband a year after that.

THE MESSAGE MAKES SENSE!

Finally I understood the message about America that my grandfather had given me years ago—this truly felt like home and made me happy. But one day, before I left my husband, he had announced that he wanted us to move to another country. The kids and I wanted to stay. That wasn't the only source of discord in our lives. He had a drinking problem that was becoming worse, and in reality, we'd had marital problems for a long time. With my awakening I had changed, and he didn't like the person I had become. I was more confident, and I wanted to have choices about my own future. The last straw came when I became a reverend of the Universal Life Church, which embraces all religions and faiths and believes we are all children of the same universe. After that, my husband said he regretted marrying me and having a family.

Needless to say, this was a very difficult time in my life, but my grandfather reminded me of his visit in a dream, and on rare occasions, the Pleiadians showed me a possible future that held peace and joy. So I found the courage to leave my husband, and the children and I embarked on our new life. I consider this decision, which required stepping into the unknown with complete faith, as one of the greatest gifts of my lifetime.

LIGHTS OF THE UNIVERSE

Around that same time I progressed from automatic writing to telepathic communication. Keneau introduced me to other guides who called themselves the Lights of the Universe. Some of them had an energy imprint similar to Keneau's and some were different, but I understood that they all wanted love and peace for us. From that time on I would communicate with the whole collective energy instead of just Keneau. He kept assisting me with my personal journey, while the Lights of the Universe assisted with the clients I worked with. They guided me to start an energy-healing group where I would send healing to the group at particular times, and they also shared messages with the group.

DNA ACTIVATION

During my sessions, when a client was interested in developing his or her psychic abilities, the guides would come and, instead of teaching about psychic development, sometimes they would elaborate on the individual's soul origin and teach us about other star nations and their signature energy and abilities. The Lights of the Universe gave me steps to use for psychic attunement, and I realized that I was working with twelve strands of DNA, addressing both the physical and the spiritual bodies. So what started as psychic development became DNA activation. The Lights of the Universe would join us in sessions and my clients made connections with their star soul families. I saw changes taking place in those clients, especially in developing their psychic and healing abilities. Some clients who were initially afraid of extraterrestrials began to accept that they share their DNA.

The Lights of the Universe explained that they collaborate with benevolent extraterrestrial beings from numerous star nations and guide them to our sessions. I trusted them. While practicing the DNA activations I slowly learned from my guides all about energy implant removals and the different kinds of negative soul energies that can affect us. In a way, the Lyme disease I suffered opened a door for me. I found the strength to make changes in my life, and my guides were right there assisting me and teaching me. I needed to work so that I could support my family, and by following my guides' advice, I was able to turn my beloved hobby into a real practice.

THE LANGUAGE OF LIGHT

I was already living in Chicago and remarried to a man who fully supported who I was, when one day at the end of a session my client told me, "I have a message for you. You can speak the Language of Light." And then she began to speak to me in the Language of Light. My heart swelled and my emotions were pouring through and I started to cry, for that was the language I'd spoken upon meeting Keneau. Then my client said, "Speak back to me." I was hesitant, but she was adamant, and as I spoke I heard my quivering voice saying those beautiful, transformative words that I could not understand.

Later that afternoon I told a friend about the experience, and he also wanted me to speak to him in the Language of Light. What happened next was surprising. As I spoke to him he started to cry the way I had when Keneau had initially appeared. He called me a few hours later and said that he had cried for a very long time. It was a good healing cry that helped him to release some bottled up emotions. He shared with me that he had not cried like that in ages, and it made him feel wonderful.

I became curious. Would it have the same effect on others? Unexpectedly, I felt the urge to speak the Language of Light to anyone who was willing to listen. Some people cried and some didn't, but I noticed a significant improvement in my clients' healing, especially in the area of emotional healing. I was grateful, although I still couldn't find much information on the Language of Light. That changed some time later when I read in the *Book of Knowledge: The Keys of Enoch* written by James J. Hurtak that this language is the language of gods, which meant to me the language of our ancient alien ancestors.

A few short months after that, the Lights of the Universe suggested that I record two meditations in the Language of Light so that anyone could use them despite language barriers. On the day of the recordings I was a little nervous but also excited about the opportunity. The equipment was set up in my house and we only had a specific window of time to complete the recordings. I was convinced that the Lights of the Universe would just come and speak through me and that it would be easy—but nothing happened the way I expected it would.

As soon as I put the headset on a few short minutes before the recording was to begin, I heard my guides telepathically say, "We will not speak through you, you can remember it now, speak from your heart, from your soul. You are ready."

I freaked out. Should I speak from my heart? There was not much time to think. I could either cancel or give it a try, so I gave it a try. I stepped aside from my logical mind and my ego. I became fully present in the moment, and then I began to speak from the heart. As the sentences were forming, tears rolled down my cheeks. I could remember it now; I felt my Pleiadian soul.

The Language of Light becomes available to us as we evolve and are able to access the higher dimensions. There our language changes from being simply a vibration of sound to one that operates on an expanded frequency. It acts as a powerful carrier of wisdom and higher dimensional energies. It cannot be translated word-for-word; each word carries a different energy. You can repeat the same word and the meaning will change when the energy changes. The Language of Light is a combination of energy, color, sacred geometric shapes, and sound. The people who speak it give it a voice and they carry its frequency.

All who speak the Language of Light today sound very different from each other, depending on their past-life incarnations, their Earth missions, and the star nations they come from. We have different dialects and each of us carries a different energy imprint to serve our soul groups. When the soul groups start working together without prejudice and have a united goal for peace, the Language of Light will combine into one language, at which point we will be ready for the next step in our collective transformation. We do not know how long that will take.

For now, the Language of Light is used for the purpose of soul healing. When your soul heals, you can remember the ancient times. You can remember all the amazing star nations—including the Pleiadians, the magnificent inventions, and your true soul power—without fear that we as humanity might self-destruct with the knowledge that will be available to us. Miraculous healings of the physical body will be common knowledge, and physical immortality will someday become a personal choice.

Of course I initially questioned whether or not the Language of Light was really of the light. In my work, I encourage people to find logical explanations to what they feel and experience, and to test the energy they are connecting with. I discourage them from blindly following anyone or anything. Once I began using the Language of Light, my personal soul growth increased. While working with my clients I would have visions about how to tailor their healing sessions. I would see symbols, which I applied in the sessions. With this, the majority of my clients would heal or improve. I had my own proof that the Language of Light was real and transformational. However, not everyone would heal and I learned a valuable lesson—that we can heal only when our soul is ready to heal. Some are absolutely ready, and some need more time. We need to respect that.

ON WORKING WITH
THE PLEIADIANS

Meeting Keneau, the Pleiadian being of light, changed me, and I am grateful for that. I began to celebrate being different, and I knew that I am here to help others understand that being different is a gift that needs to be used in the present time to make this world a better place for the generations to come.

The Lights of the Universe would guide me through self-discovery of my past lives. I regained faint memories of lives in Lemuria, Atlantis, and Egypt. In a vision I was guided to make a symbol that worked as an amplifier of my energy work. Later on I stumbled upon a documentary on Egypt and learned that the symbol was the ankh, a real tool that Egyptian gods used. I've had many instances where I've been guided toward something and then later I find recorded information about it. It works as an affirmation for me that I am not simply formulating this myself. We have soul memories and we cannot make up something we have not experienced before. In our current human evolution we are still far behind what our soul already knows.

The Lights of the Universe guided me in writing. Just as Keneau was urging me to learn energy healing, they urged me to write. At first I thought writing was just a dream, one that I couldn't manifest, because English is my second language. They, however, were persistent, and I am grateful that I can share their energy through my writings with you.

I hope you have noticed that while you read the channeled descriptions of the different star nations you are making contact with their energy. Since they are your stellar family, they shared with me that they will fine-tune your energy and activate your sleeping DNA so the healing process can begin and unfold into the original twelve fully functioning strands. Our stellar families desire to assist you in the highest possible way in your current life here on Earth.

For years I would experience moments of sleep paralysis, which can be a very frightening experience for any starseed. One night I woke up completely paralyzed with energy. My whole body was vibrating and I felt like I was hovering above the bed. Instead of fighting the fear I calmed myself within, and I called upon my guides to show me if they were the instigators of this and whether or not this was happening for my highest good instead of just assuming it was a negative experience. To my utter surprise, I felt my guides asking me to trust them and that yes, they were involved in this.

So I relaxed and surrendered to the unusual experience. It felt as if my body was vibrating even faster. I felt myself floating above the bed, and then in an instant it was over and I never experienced it again. Strangely, I felt really good afterward.

Another interesting experience came while I was meditating. I remember being pulled quickly through what I can only describe as a black hole, and into an unknown place. I did not know where I was; I think it may have been a spaceship. Then I remember a voice telling me, "Now you are ready to go back. Scream at the top of your lungs because that will lower your vibration and you will get back into your body."

So I began to scream, and then felt myself moving extremely quickly into the physical body. It was in the middle of the night and upon hearing me, my husband, who was working late in our home office, ran into the room, fearing that something horrible was going on. He asked me what had happened and the only answer I could give him was that I had been on a spaceship. It felt amazing. I found it interesting that screaming lowers our vibration and activates the fear and survival mode that's connected to the physical body. Living with aliens makes life interesting when you lose your fear of the unknown and you learn to trust them and follow your intuition.

We moved to South Carolina in 2015 and we're still here. It was a great decision to move! I was guided to move close to the thirty-third parallel, which is aligned with Alcyone, in the Pleiades constellation. I can also feel connected to the ancient Atlantean energy that radiates here. It amplifies everything and either brings out the best or the worst in you; there is nothing in-between. When I learned to trust that the universe has my back, my life became easier.

I began to experience alignments with my higher self, which is closely connected to the Pleiadians. She goes and visits people in dreams or meditations and heals and offers guidance, often without my conscious knowledge. I have heard this from others who claim they have seen me during a healing or while in a meditative state hundreds of miles away from where I actually am, which always amazes me.

I also found a true teacher in the physical realm. I began to work on healing my pain body, my emotional body, and my own soul's PTSD. You have to heal the human part of your being so you can connect with the alien within. One night I experienced a dark night of the soul (one of several I have experienced in this lifetime) I thought I was doing pretty well, so this one surprised me.

Without any warning sign I faced the dark energies, or the dark monster, I'd been afraid of my whole life. I had a moment of clarity and knew that this dark form that had often affected me since childhood was actually a collection of my own fears. I had created it and I had to face it, myself, alone, in the middle of the darkness of the night. I surrendered and I prayed and I forgave and eventually before the sun came out, still surrounded by the darkness of the night, I felt unconditional love. I felt peace. I was connected to everything that there is, which I call God.

And then the Pleiadians said, "It is time for you to write." And that is how it all began, and why I became an author of books about spirituality, healing, and extraterrestrials.

Believe in yourself!

I wish you Love and Light on your journey.

Eva Marquez

About the Author

Eva Marquez is a spiritual counselor and healer, teacher, and writer. In her spiritual work she utilizes her inherited Pleiadian energy. She remembers the Language of Light along with many other ancient soul memories and works with her guides, the Lights of the Universe, who are a collective group of light beings from various star nations. She also works with her higher self who, on occasion, enjoys visiting others in dreams and during meditation to give assistance or healing if needed.

Eva's mission is to teach you about your personal powers so that you can be your own guru! She also brings back memories of infinite love from God. Love is the most important energy tool we each have. She is dedicated to assisting those who need healing on all levels.

Eva works with people who have terminal illness, mothers who are expecting a child with birth defects, those who have fallen into deep depression or despair, those who have lost all hope, those who are suffocated by fear, those who feel all alone, those who have been abused both physically and mentally, and anyone else needing assistance and guidance. She works through ancient DNA and assists starseeds in connecting with their soul families and activating their DNA and their memories. She is here to show you that there is a "light at the end of the tunnel" and that through love we can reach that light.

✳ ✳ ✳

Learn more about Eva and her services at www.EvaMarquez.org and visit her YouTube channel for free healing, meditations, and spiritual guidance: Eva Marquez on YouTube.

Index